Max Axiom and the Society of Super Scientists

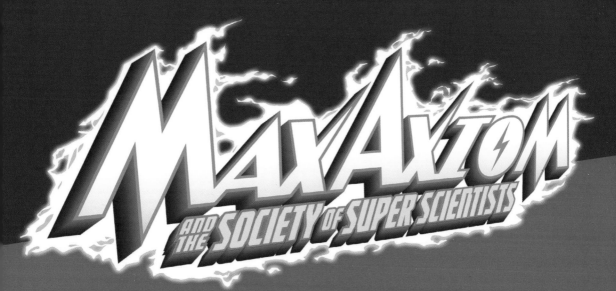

Exploring the Solar System and Beyond

by Ailynn Collins
illustrated by Erik Doescher

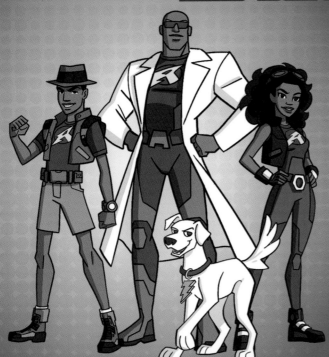

CAPSTONE PRESS
a capstone imprint

Published by Capstone Press, an imprint of Capstone.
1710 Roe Crest Drive North Mankato, Minnesota 56003
capstonepub.com

Library of Congress Cataloging-in-Publication Data
is available on the Library of Congress website.
ISBN: 9781666337105 (hardcover)
ISBN: 9781666337112 (paperback)
ISBN: 9781666337129 (eBook PDF)

Summary: Since the 1960s, several probes, orbiters, landers, and rovers
have explored the planets and their moons. What incredible discoveries
were made during these daring missions? And what will be needed for
humans to visit the planets in person? Ride along with Max Axiom and
the Society of Super Scientists to learn about the solar system and the risks
involved in traveling to the planets and beyond.

Editorial Credits
Editor: Aaron Sautter; Designer: Brann Garvey; Media Researcher: Morgan
Walters; Production Specialist: Polly Fisher

All internet sites appearing in back matter were available and accurate
when this book was sent to press.

Printed and bound in the USA. PO4882

TABLE OF CONTENTS

SECTION 1:
A SURPRISE 6

SECTION 2:
SPACE TRAVEL TODAY 8

SECTION 3:
SPACE TRAVEL IN THE FUTURE 14

SECTION 4:
BEYOND THE MOON AND MARS 18

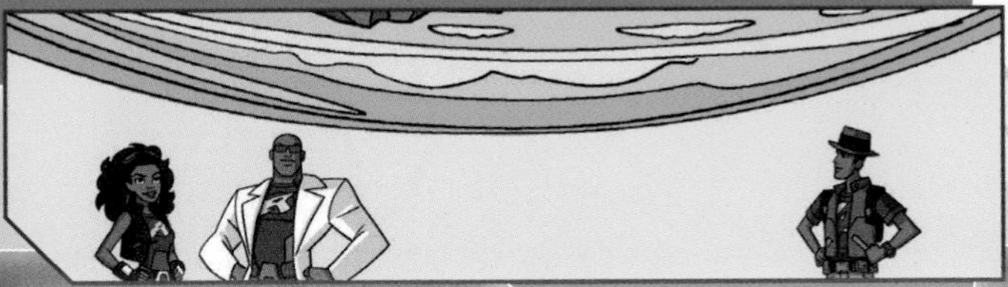

THE FUTURE OF SPACE EXPLORATION	28
GLOSSARY	30
READ MORE	31
INTERNET SITES	31
INDEX	32
ABOUT THE AUTHOR	32

THE SOCIETY OF SUPER SCIENTISTS

MAX AXIOM

After years of study, Max Axiom, the world's first Super Scientist, knew the mysteries of the universe were too vast for one person alone to uncover. So Max created the Society of Super Scientists! Using their superpowers and super-smarts, this talented group investigates today's most urgent scientific and environmental issues and learns about actions everyone can take to solve them.

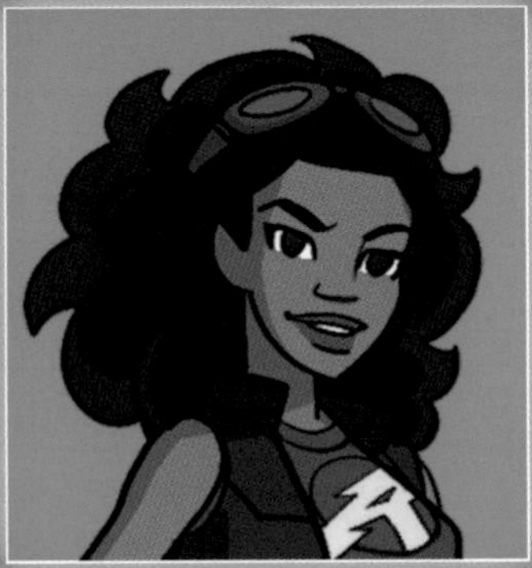

LIZZY AXIOM

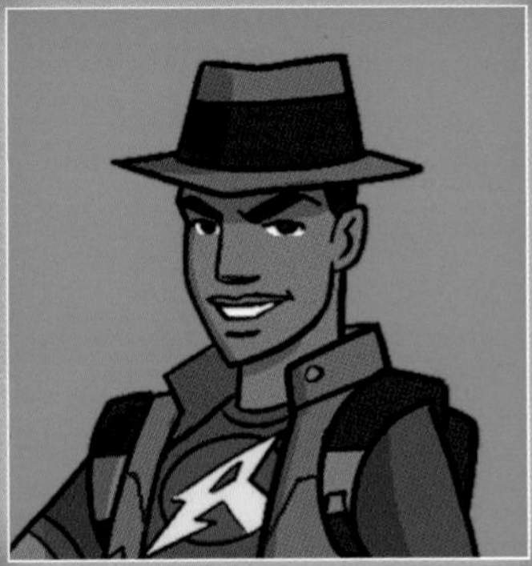

NICK AXIOM

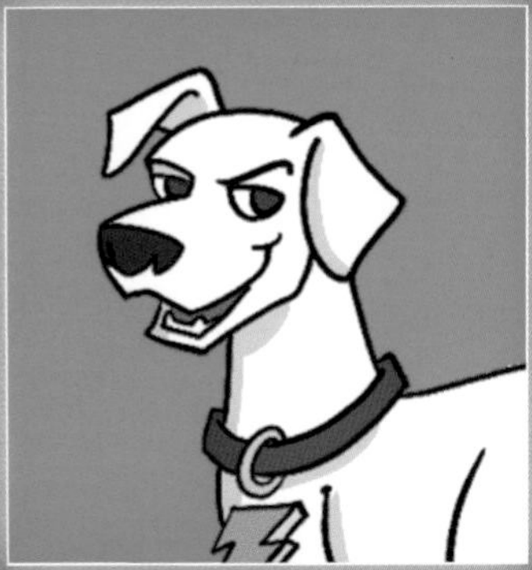

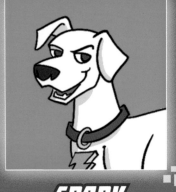

SPARK

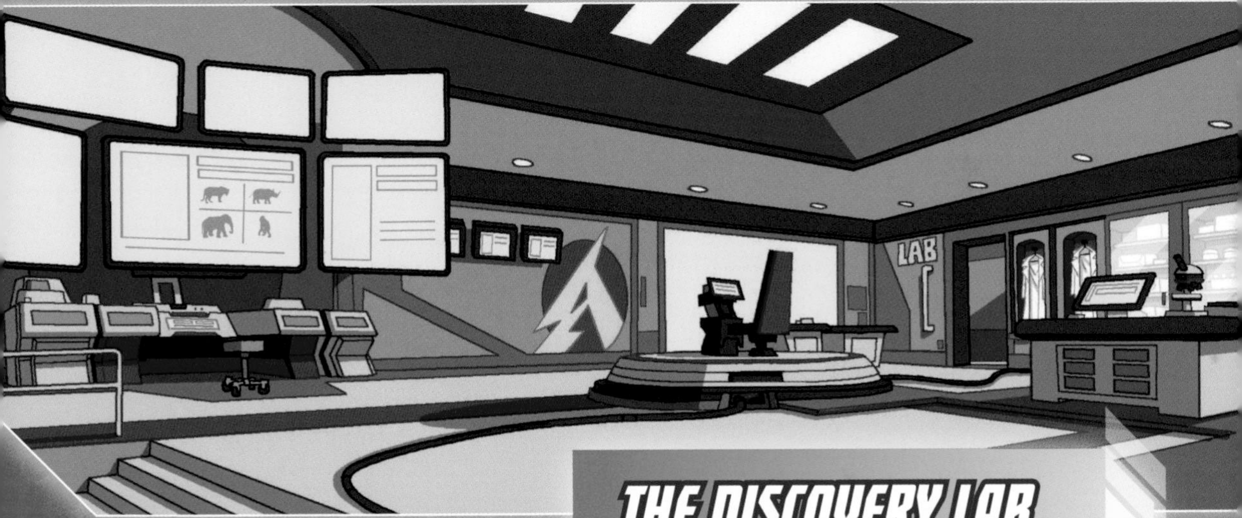
LAB

THE DISCOVERY LAB

Home of the Society of Super Scientists, this state-of-the-art lab houses advanced tools for cutting-edge research and radical scientific innovation. More importantly, it is a space for Super Scientists to collaborate and share knowledge as they work together to tackle any challenge.

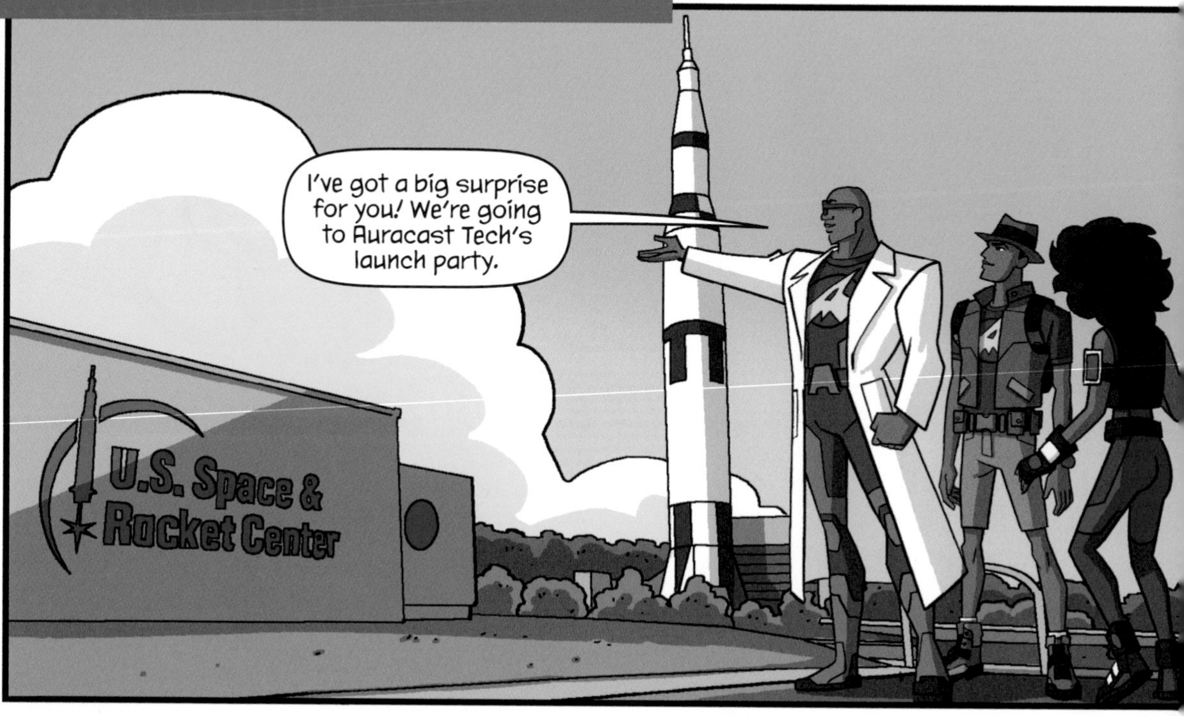
I've got a big surprise for you! We're going to Auracast Tech's launch party.
U.S. Space & Rocket Center

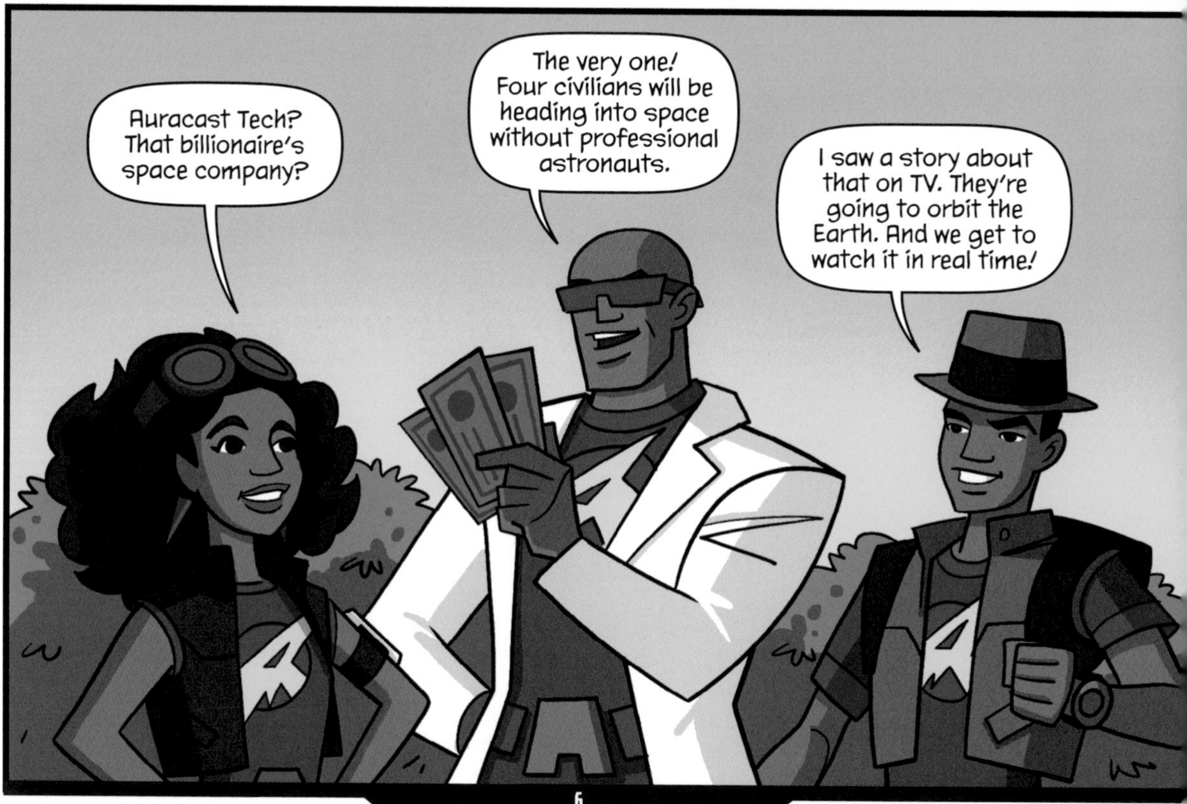
Auracast Tech? That billionaire's space company?
The very one! Four civilians will be heading into space without professional astronauts.
I saw a story about that on TV. They're going to orbit the Earth. And we get to watch it in real time!

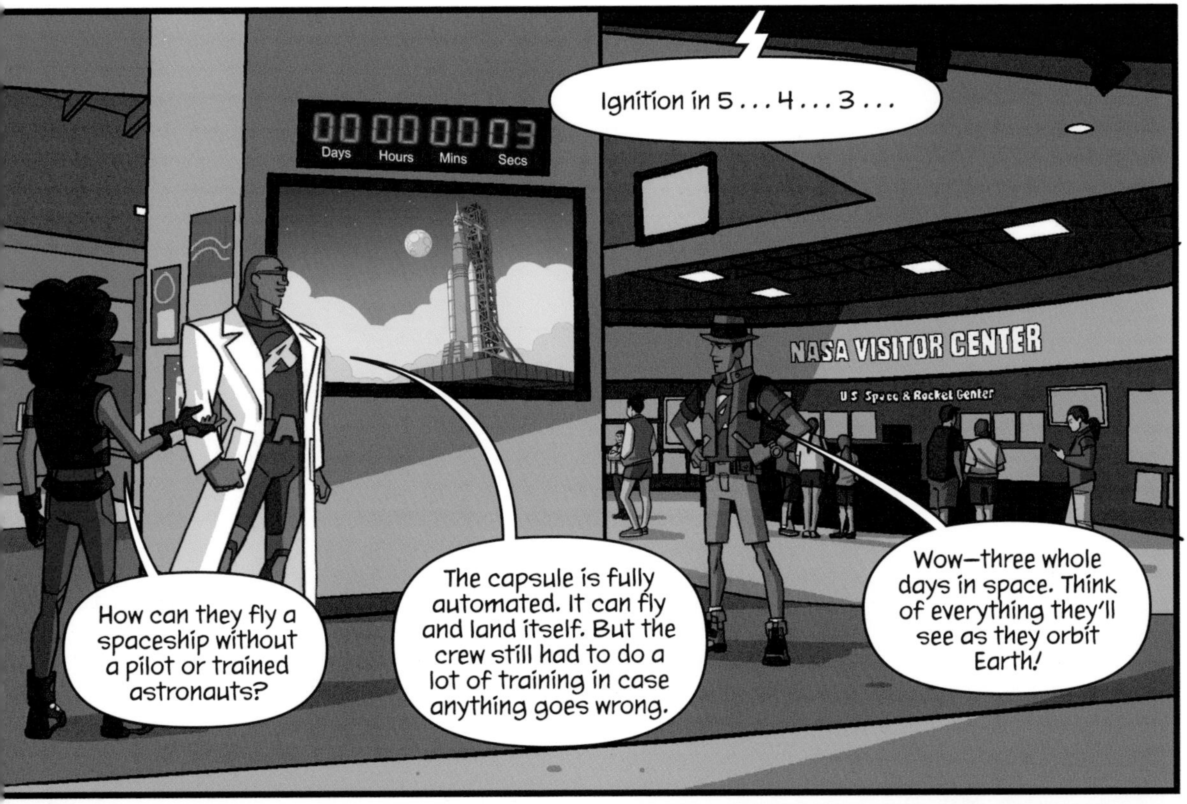
00 00 00 03
Days Hours Mins Secs
Ignition in 5 . . . 4 . . . 3 . . .
NASA VISITOR CENTER
U.S. Space & Rocket Center
How can they fly a spaceship without a pilot or trained astronauts?
The capsule is fully automated. It can fly and land itself. But the crew still had to do a lot of training in case anything goes wrong.
Wow—three whole days in space. Think of everything they'll see as they orbit Earth!

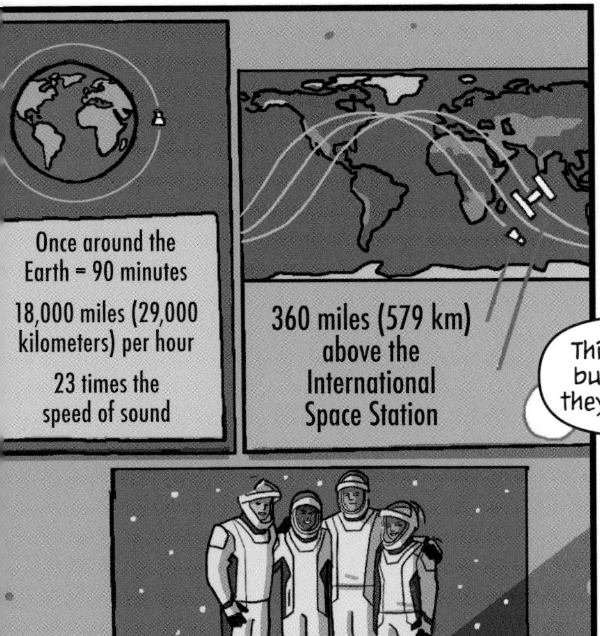
Once around the Earth = 90 minutes
18,000 miles (29,000 kilometers) per hour
23 times the speed of sound
360 miles (579 km) above the International Space Station

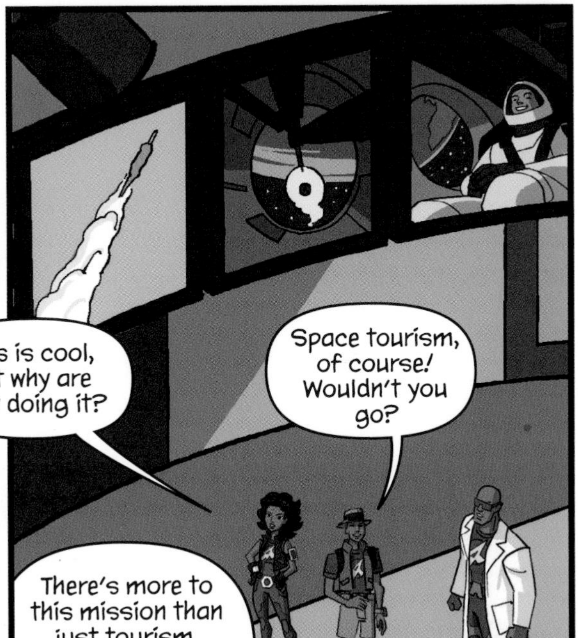
This is cool, but why are they doing it?
Space tourism, of course! Wouldn't you go?
There's more to this mission than just tourism. Let's explore this place. Maybe it'll give you some answers.

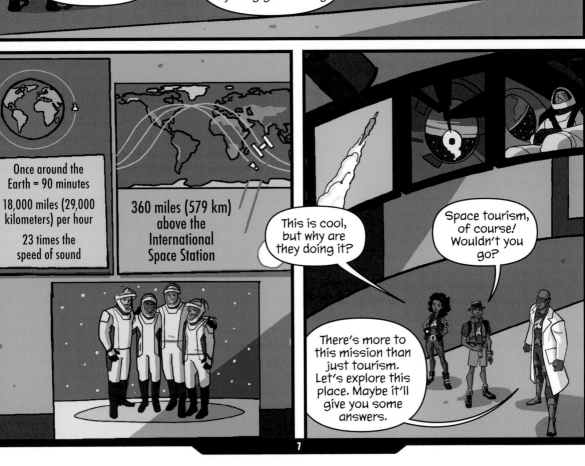

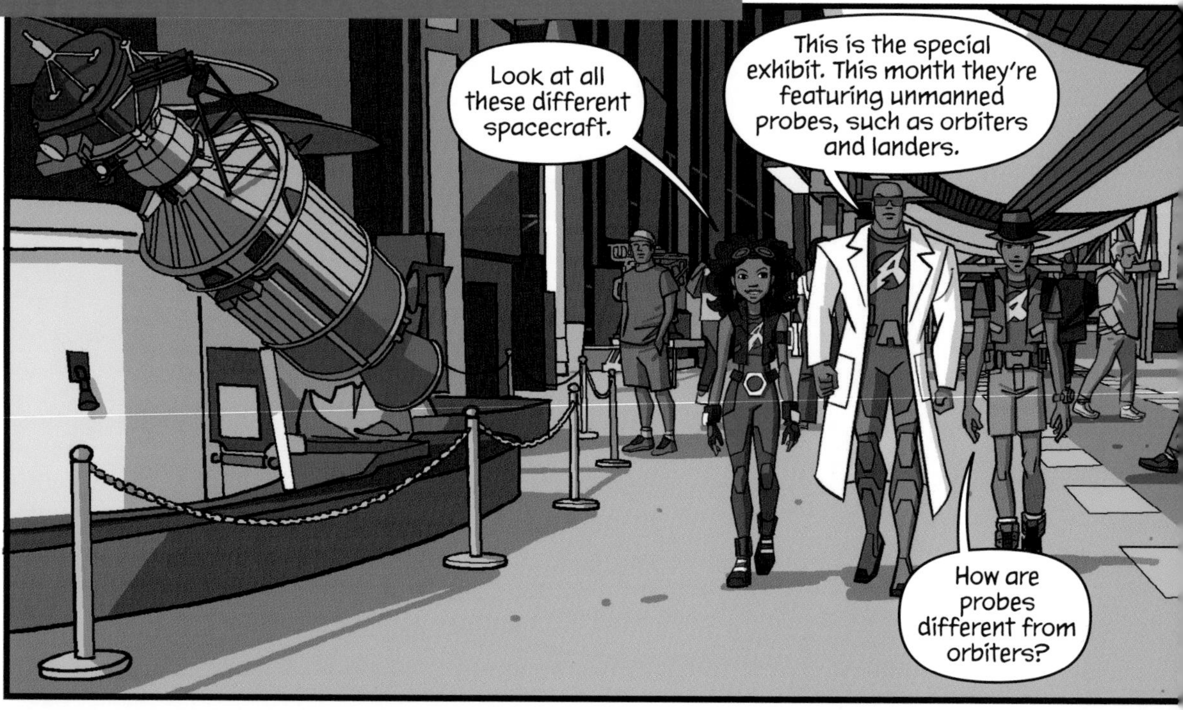
Look at all these different spacecraft.
This is the special exhibit. This month they're featuring unmanned probes, such as orbiters and landers.
How are probes different from orbiters?

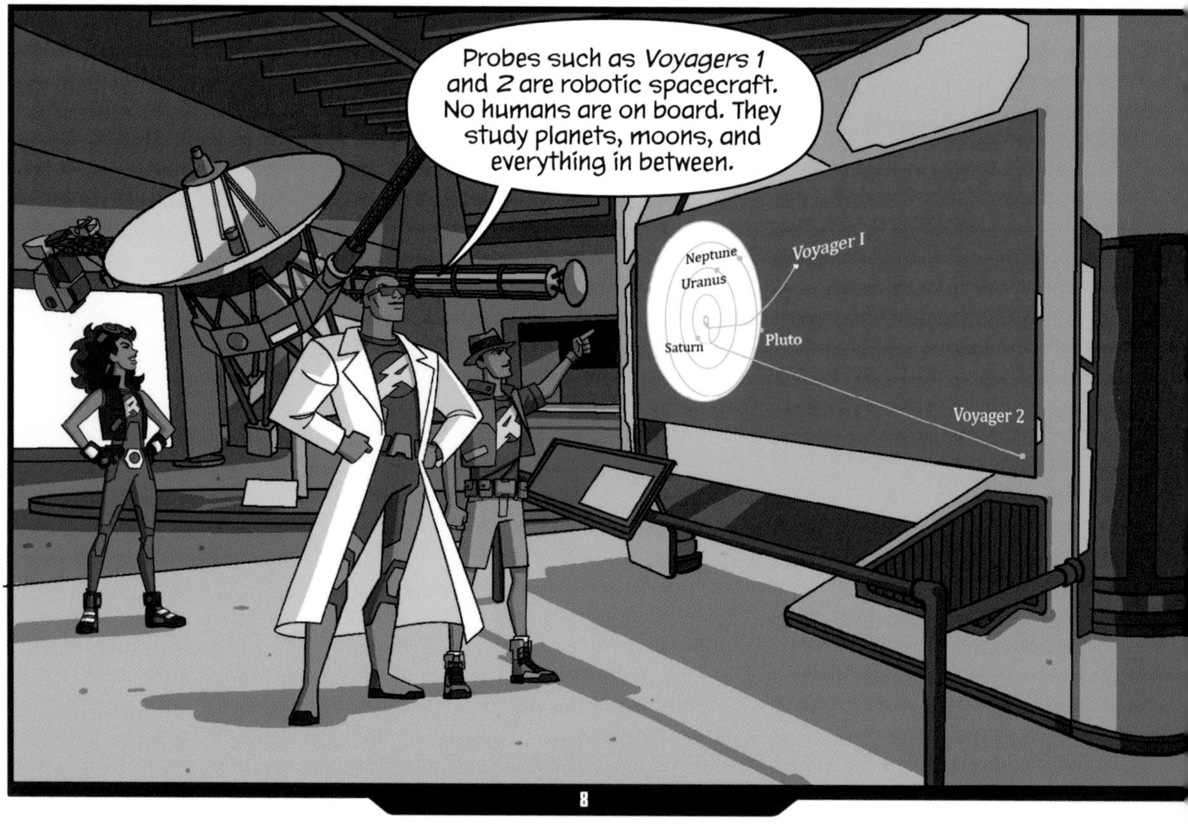
Probes such as *Voyagers 1* and *2* are robotic spacecraft. No humans are on board. They study planets, moons, and everything in between.
Neptune
Uranus
Saturn
Pluto
Voyager I
Voyager 2

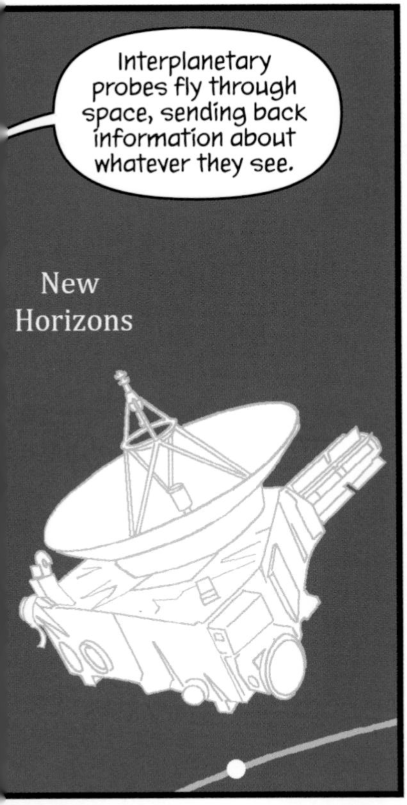
Interplanetary probes fly through space, sending back information about whatever they see.
New Horizons

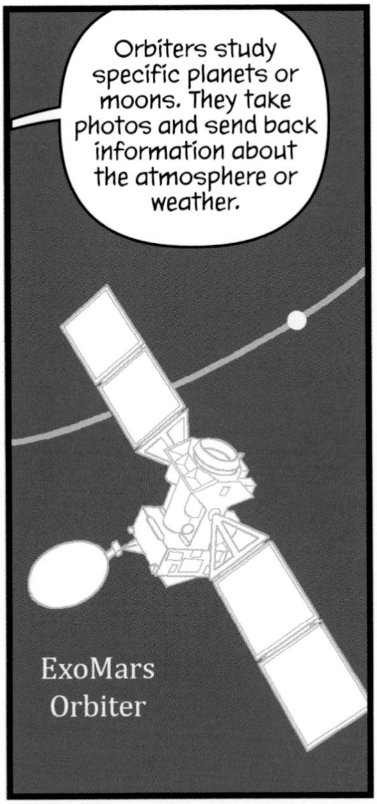
Orbiters study specific planets or moons. They take photos and send back information about the atmosphere or weather.
ExoMars Orbiter

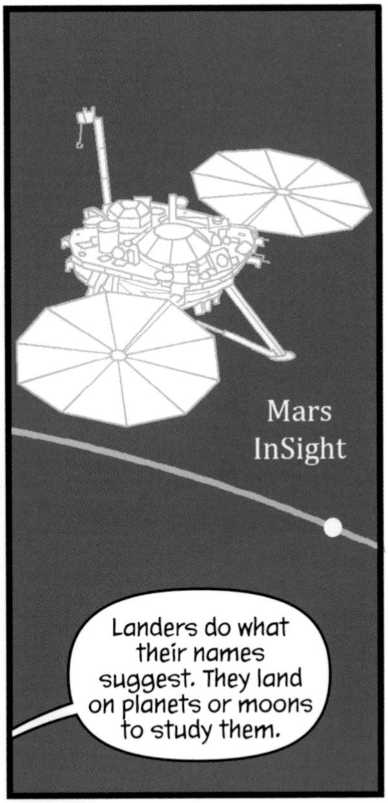
Mars InSight
Landers do what their names suggest. They land on planets or moons to study them.

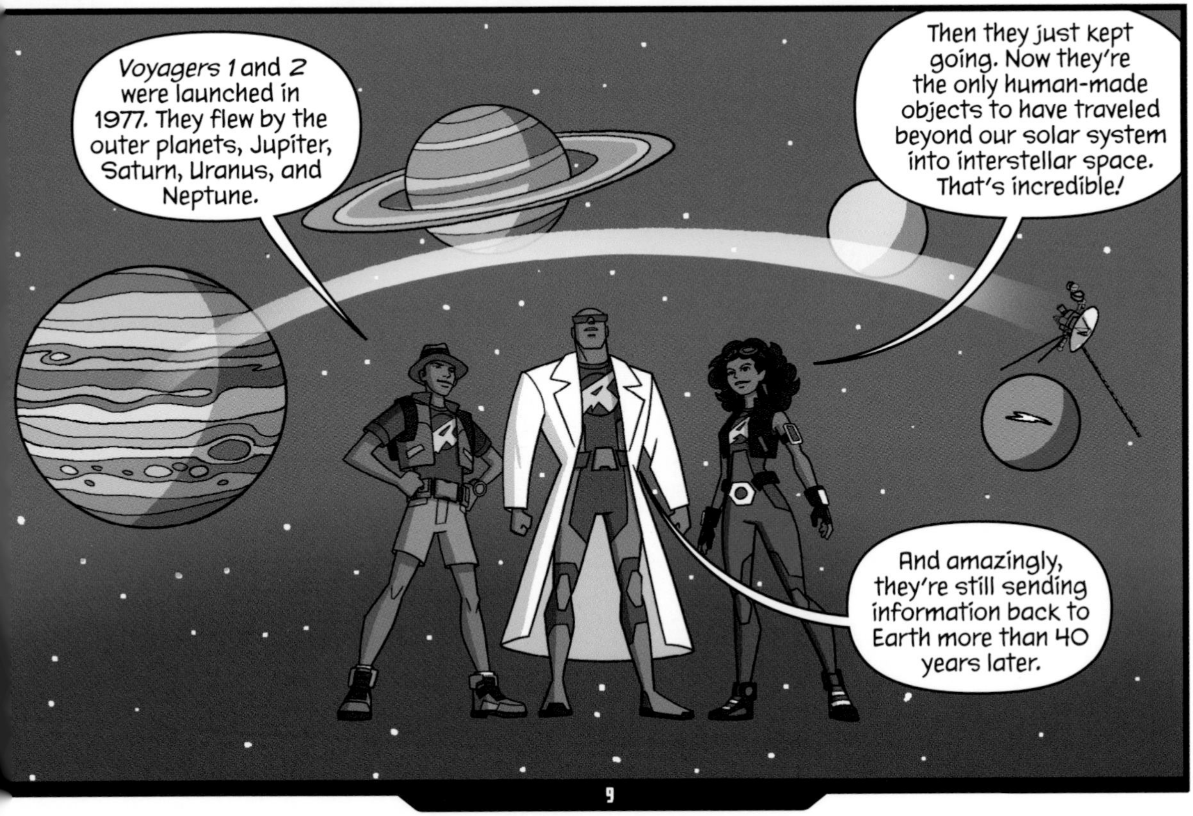
Voyagers 1 and *2* were launched in 1977. They flew by the outer planets, Jupiter, Saturn, Uranus, and Neptune.
Then they just kept going. Now they're the only human-made objects to have traveled beyond our solar system into interstellar space. That's incredible!
And amazingly, they're still sending information back to Earth more than 40 years later.

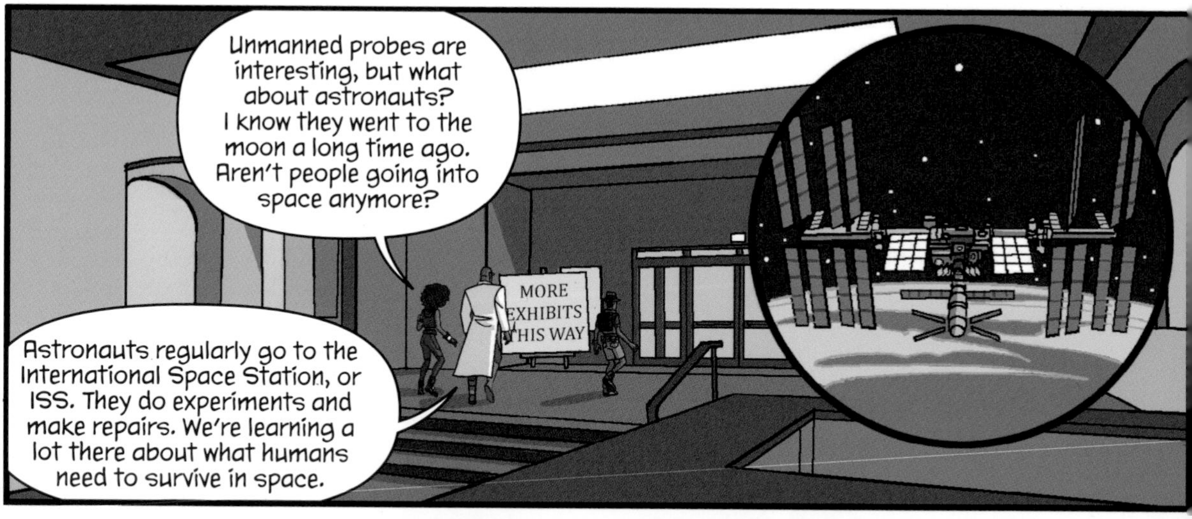
Unmanned probes are interesting, but what about astronauts? I know they went to the moon a long time ago. Aren't people going into space anymore?
MORE EXHIBITS THIS WAY
Astronauts regularly go to the International Space Station, or ISS. They do experiments and make repairs. We're learning a lot there about what humans need to survive in space.

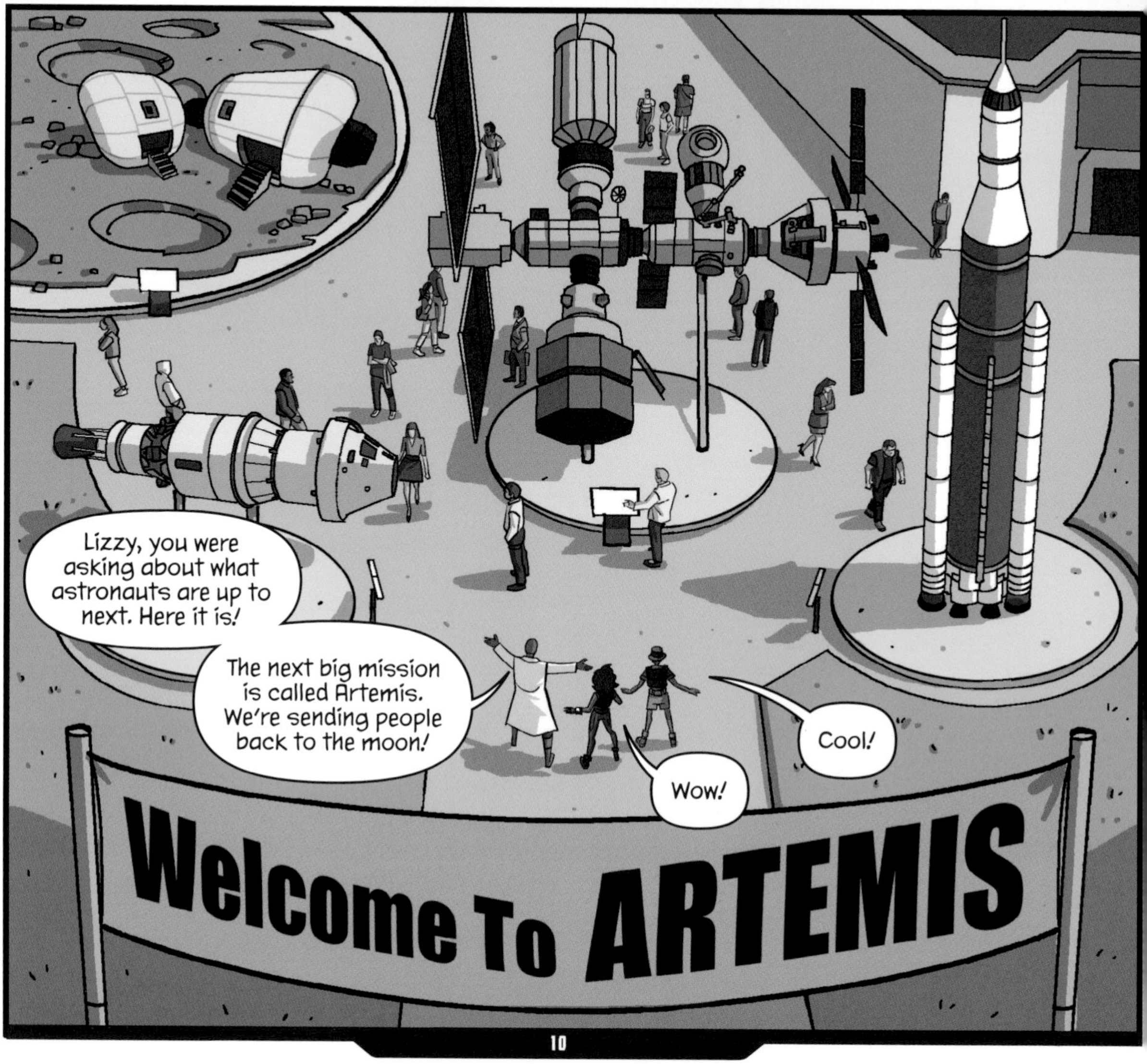
Lizzy, you were asking about what astronauts are up to next. Here it is!
The next big mission is called Artemis. We're sending people back to the moon!
Wow!
Cool!
Welcome To ARTEMIS

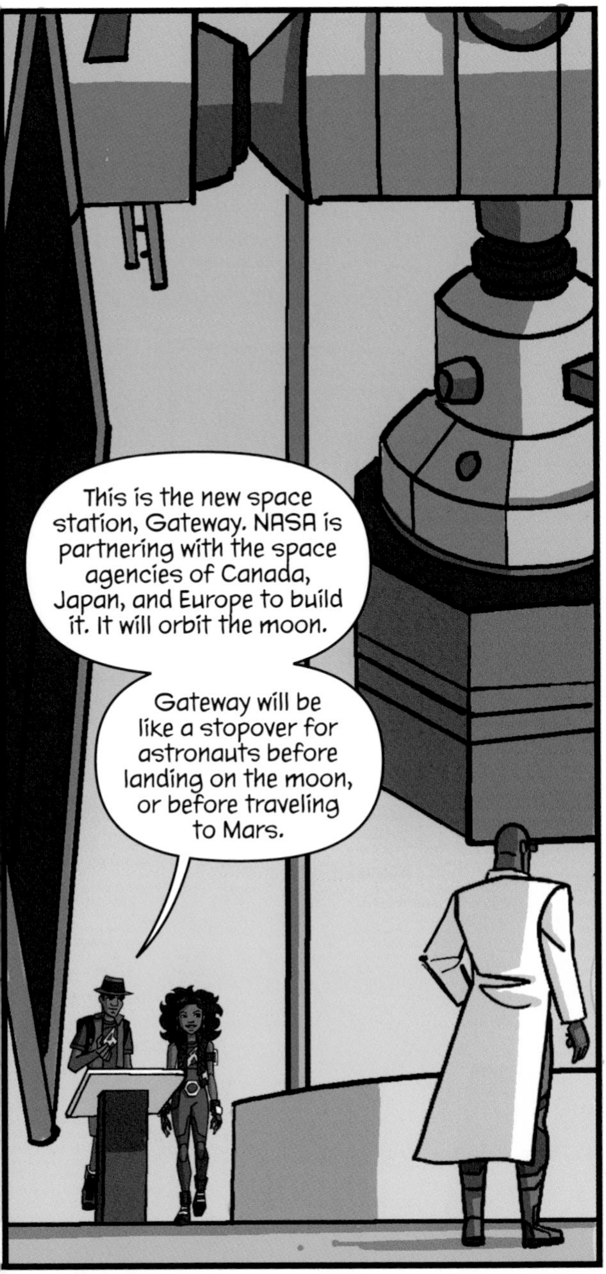
This is the new space station, Gateway. NASA is partnering with the space agencies of Canada, Japan, and Europe to build it. It will orbit the moon.
Gateway will be like a stopover for astronauts before landing on the moon, or before traveling to Mars.

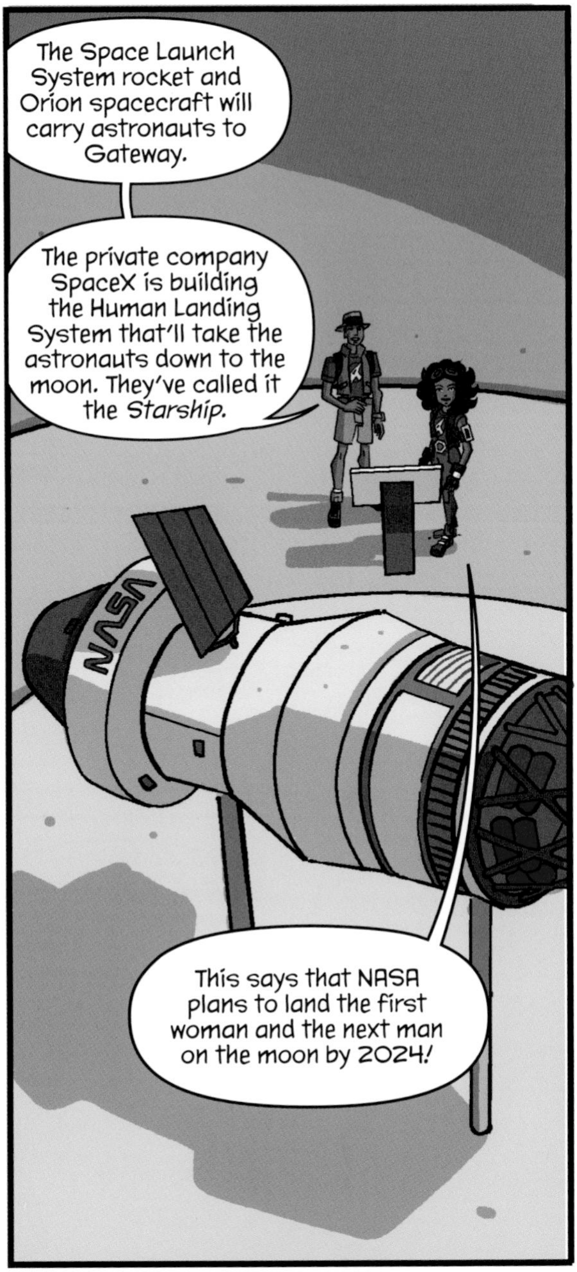
The Space Launch System rocket and Orion spacecraft will carry astronauts to Gateway.
The private company SpaceX is building the Human Landing System that'll take the astronauts down to the moon. They've called it the *Starship*.
NASA
This says that NASA plans to land the first woman and the next man on the moon by 2024!

THE ARTEMIS MISSIONS

The NASA Artemis missions will be the first to take a woman and a person of color to the moon. New technology will be used to explore more of the moon's surface than ever before. NASA will work with private companies and partner with other countries to create the first long-term presence on the moon. From there, they plan to use what they learn to take the next giant leap—sending the first astronauts to Mars.

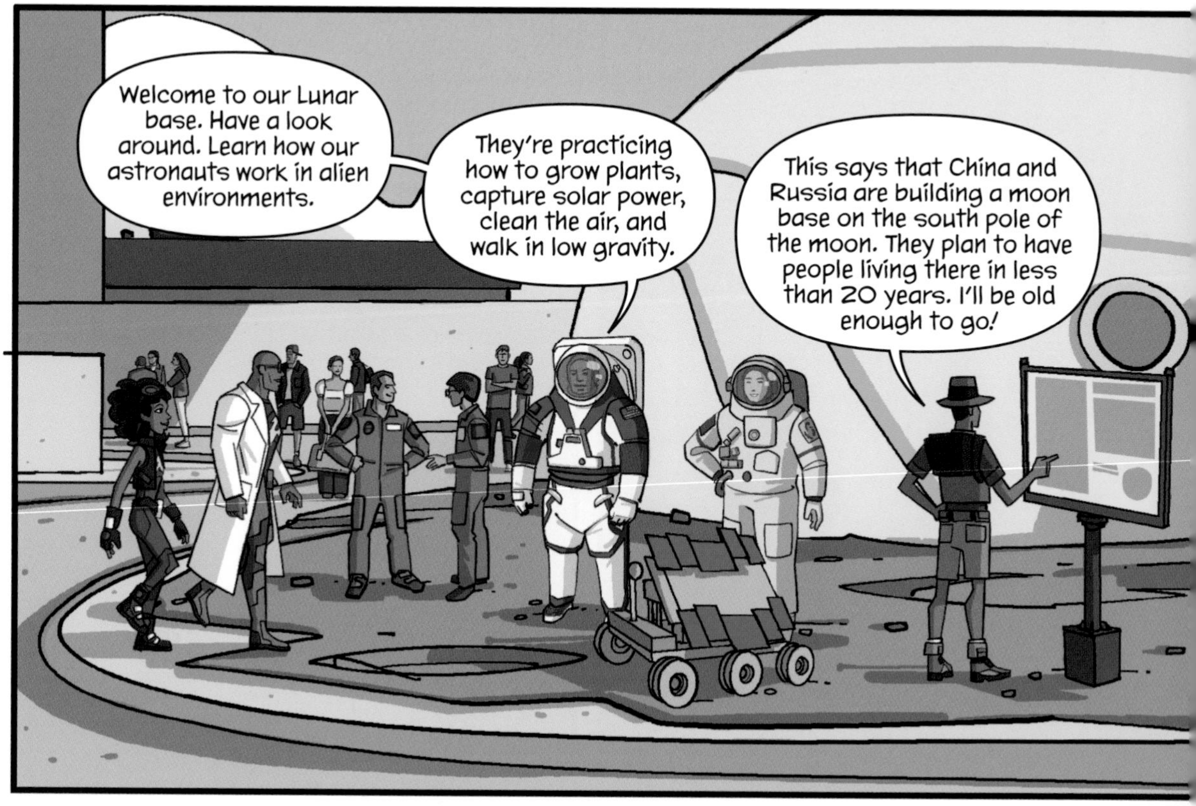
Welcome to our Lunar base. Have a look around. Learn how our astronauts work in alien environments.
They're practicing how to grow plants, capture solar power, clean the air, and walk in low gravity.
This says that China and Russia are building a moon base on the south pole of the moon. They plan to have people living there in less than 20 years. I'll be old enough to go!

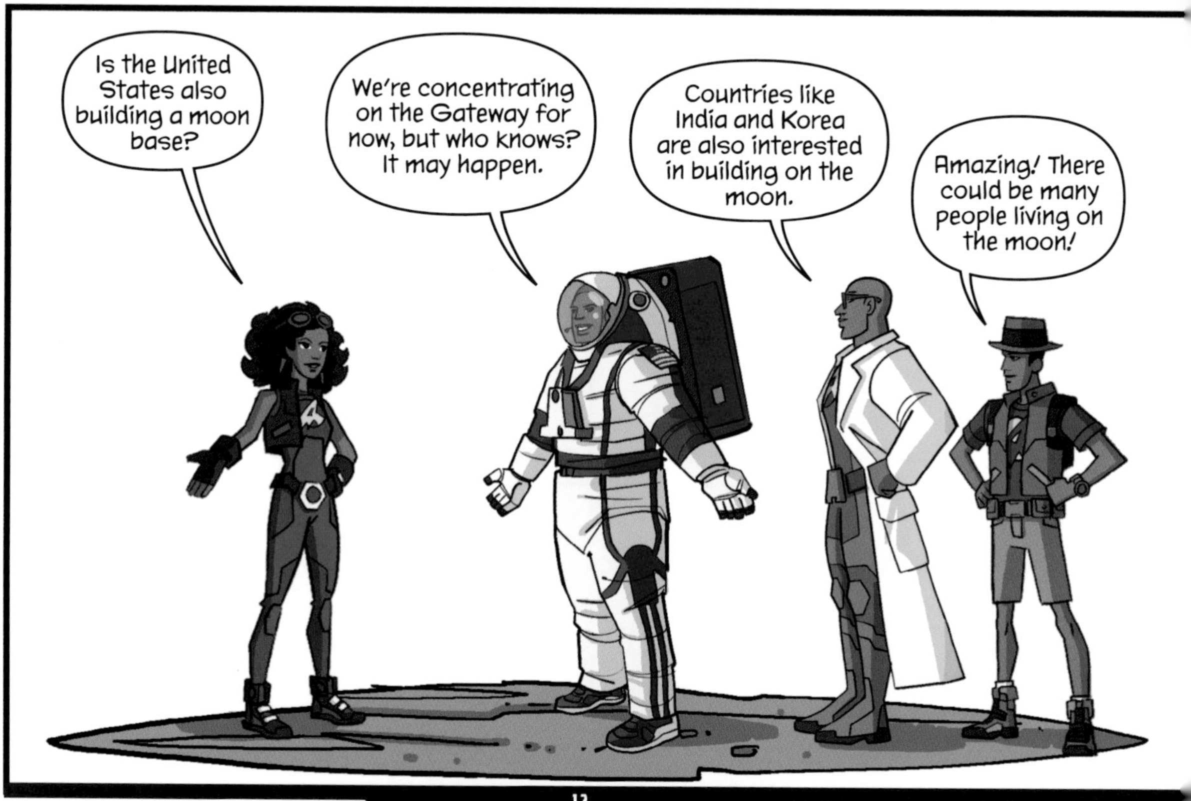
Is the United States also building a moon base?
We're concentrating on the Gateway for now, but who knows? It may happen.
Countries like India and Korea are also interested in building on the moon.
Amazing! There could be many people living on the moon!

Think about it. Someday kids will be born there too. Earth will be as strange to them as the moon is to us today.

It'll be like what we've seen in sci-fi movies!

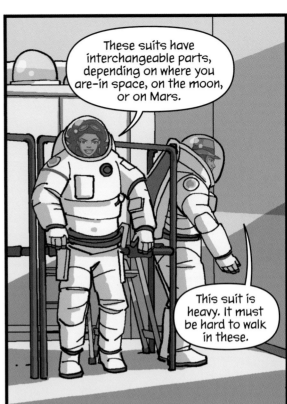

These suits have interchangeable parts, depending on where you are–in space, on the moon, or on Mars.

This suit is heavy. It must be hard to walk in these.

These are lighter copies of the latest space suits. The real ones were tested on rocky areas in the deserts in central Oregon. You can see it in this video.

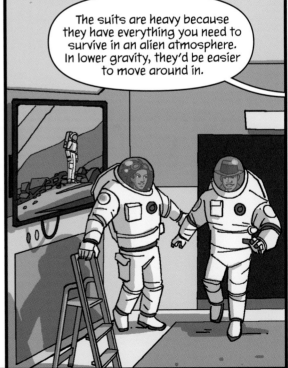

The suits are heavy because they have everything you need to survive in an alien atmosphere. In lower gravity, they'd be easier to move around in.

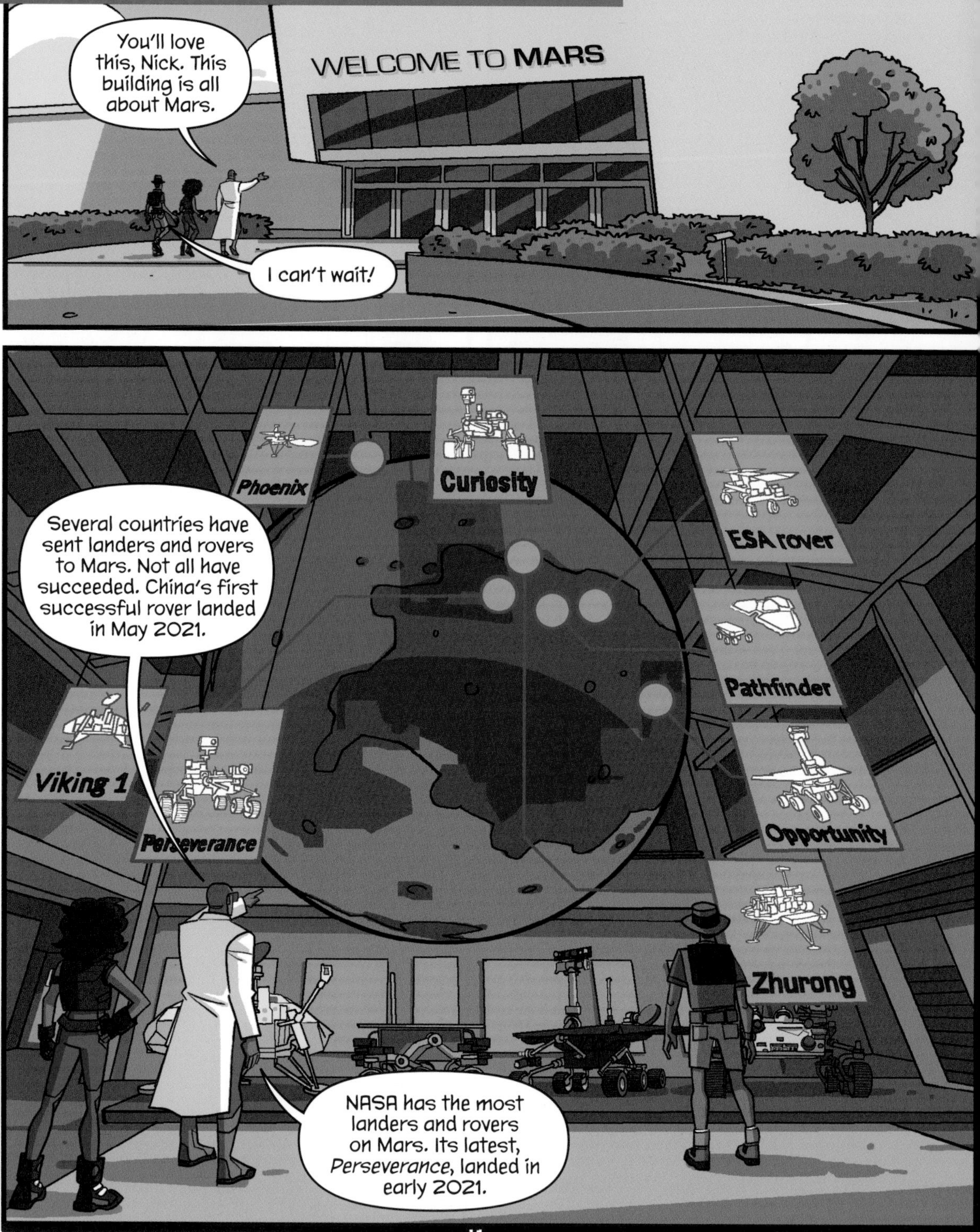
You'll love this, Nick. This building is all about Mars.
WELCOME TO MARS
I can't wait!
Phoenix
Curiosity
ESA rover
Several countries have sent landers and rovers to Mars. Not all have succeeded. China's first successful rover landed in May 2021.
Pathfinder
Viking 1
Perseverance
Opportunity
Zhurong
NASA has the most landers and rovers on Mars. Its latest, *Perseverance*, landed in early 2021.

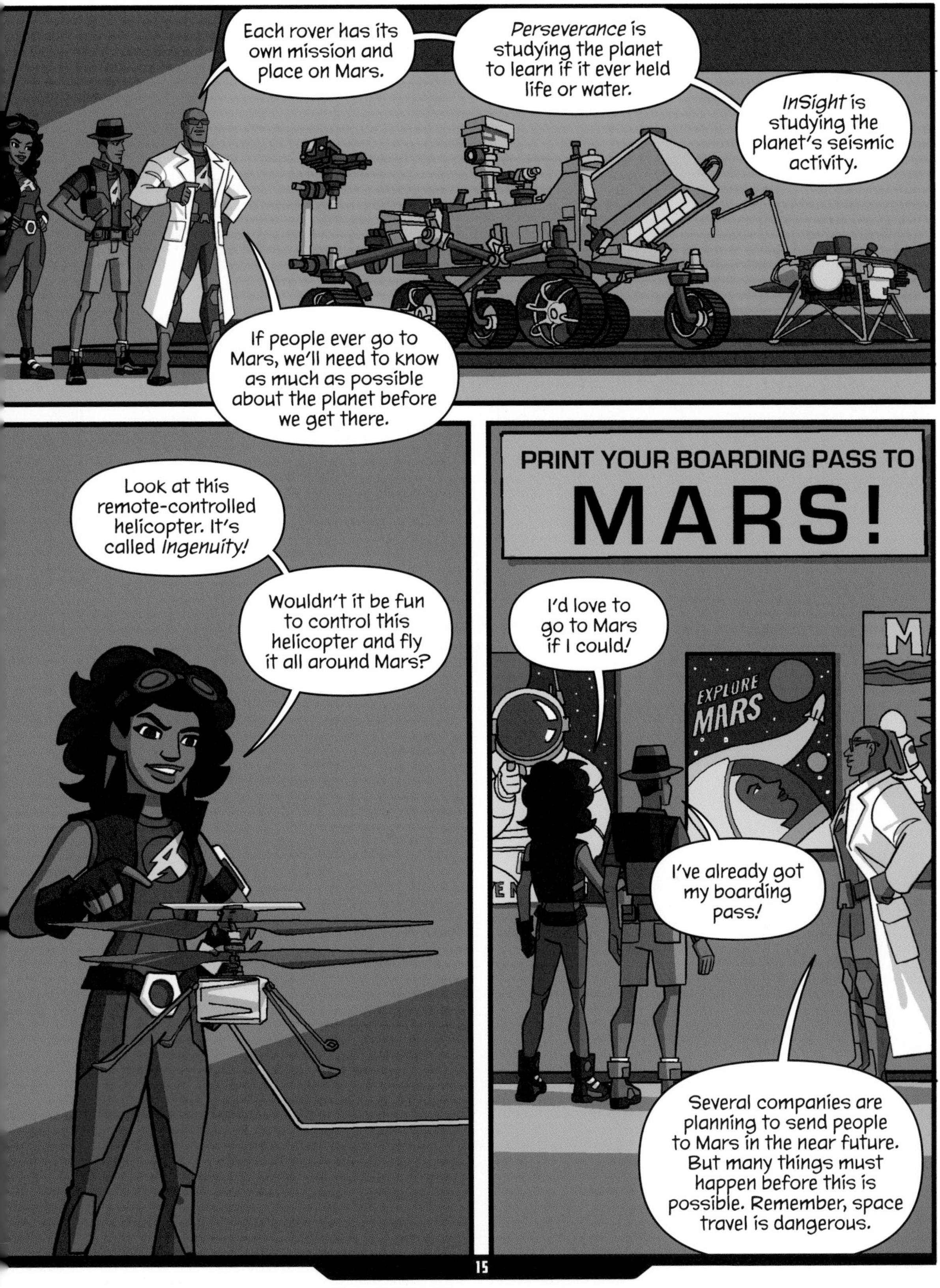
Each rover has its own mission and place on Mars.
Perseverance is studying the planet to learn if it ever held life or water.
InSight is studying the planet's seismic activity.
If people ever go to Mars, we'll need to know as much as possible about the planet before we get there.
Look at this remote-controlled helicopter. It's called *Ingenuity*!
Wouldn't it be fun to control this helicopter and fly it all around Mars?
PRINT YOUR BOARDING PASS TO
MARS!
I'd love to go to Mars if I could!
EXPLORE MARS
I've already got my boarding pass!
Several companies are planning to send people to Mars in the near future. But many things must happen before this is possible. Remember, space travel is dangerous.

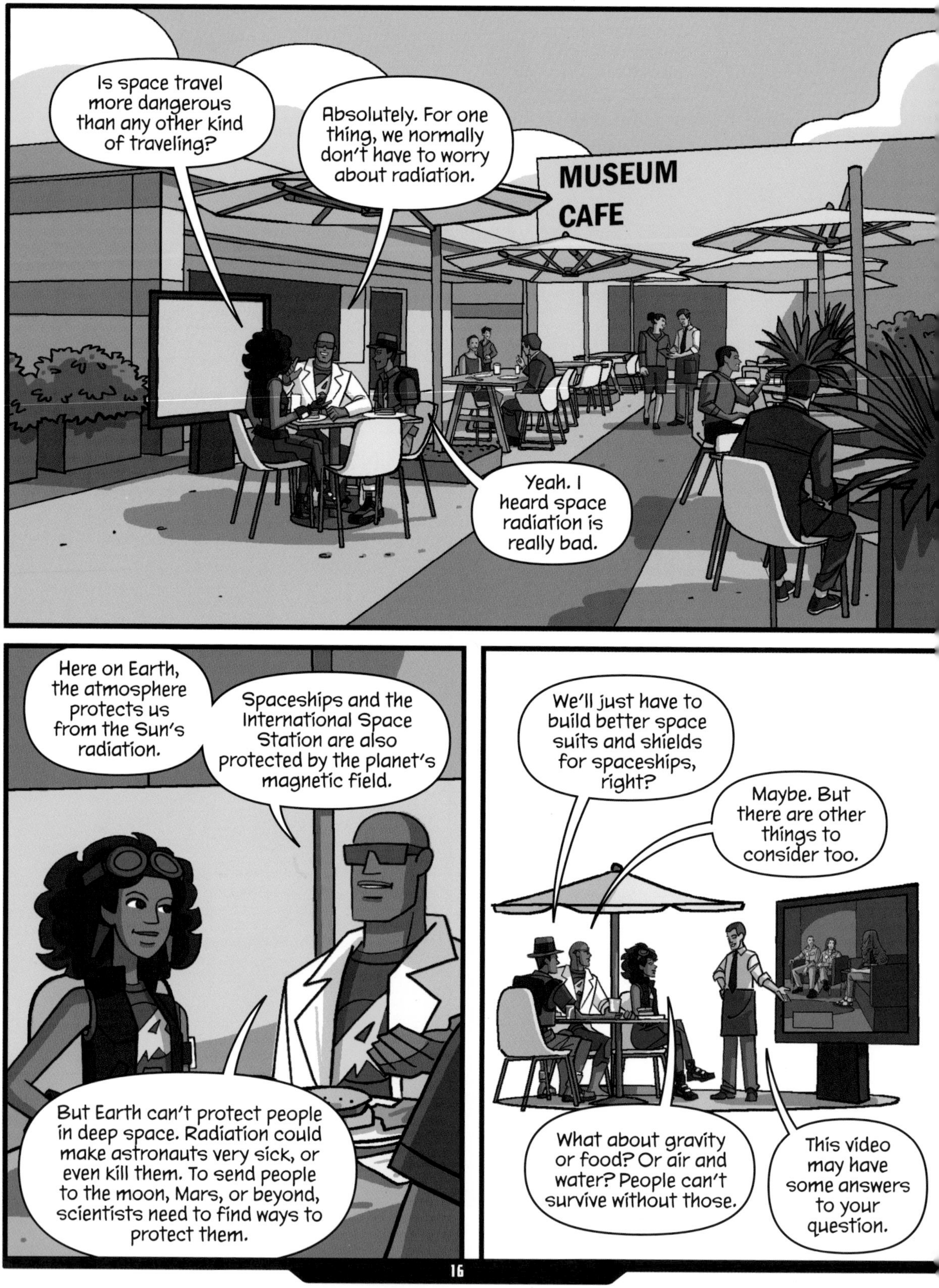
Is space travel more dangerous than any other kind of traveling?
Absolutely. For one thing, we normally don't have to worry about radiation.
MUSEUM CAFE
Yeah. I heard space radiation is really bad.
Here on Earth, the atmosphere protects us from the Sun's radiation.
Spaceships and the International Space Station are also protected by the planet's magnetic field.
But Earth can't protect people in deep space. Radiation could make astronauts very sick, or even kill them. To send people to the moon, Mars, or beyond, scientists need to find ways to protect them.
We'll just have to build better space suits and shields for spaceships, right?
Maybe. But there are other things to consider too.
What about gravity or food? Or air and water? People can't survive without those.
This video may have some answers to your question.

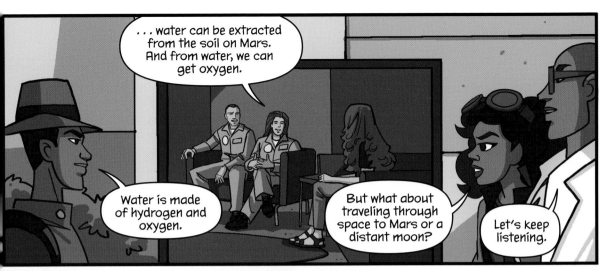

. . . water can be extracted from the soil on Mars. And from water, we can get oxygen.

Water is made of hydrogen and oxygen.

But what about traveling through space to Mars or a distant moon?

Let's keep listening.

It will take almost three years to travel to Mars and back. A crew of four would need more than 24,000 pounds, or 10,886 kilograms, of food. That and water would take up a lot of space in the ship.

Some food is dehydrated. We then add water before eating it. But in space, water is scarce, so we can't have too much of this kind of food. One solution is food bars, similar to granola bars you may have at home.

Imagine eating granola bars every day for three years!

I didn't realize there were so many things to think about with space travel.

People also need mental toughness to be gone from Earth for so long. There's still much to figure out before we head into deep space. But I have no doubt we'll get there. Let's head to the next exhibit.

RECORD BREAKING!

To travel to distant worlds, scientists need to know how space affects the human body and mind. Astronaut Scott Kelly lived on the International Space Station (ISS) for 340 days. Astronaut Mark Vande Hei returned to Earth in March 2022 after being on the ISS for more than 350 days. The experiences of these astronauts are teaching scientists a lot about long term space travel.

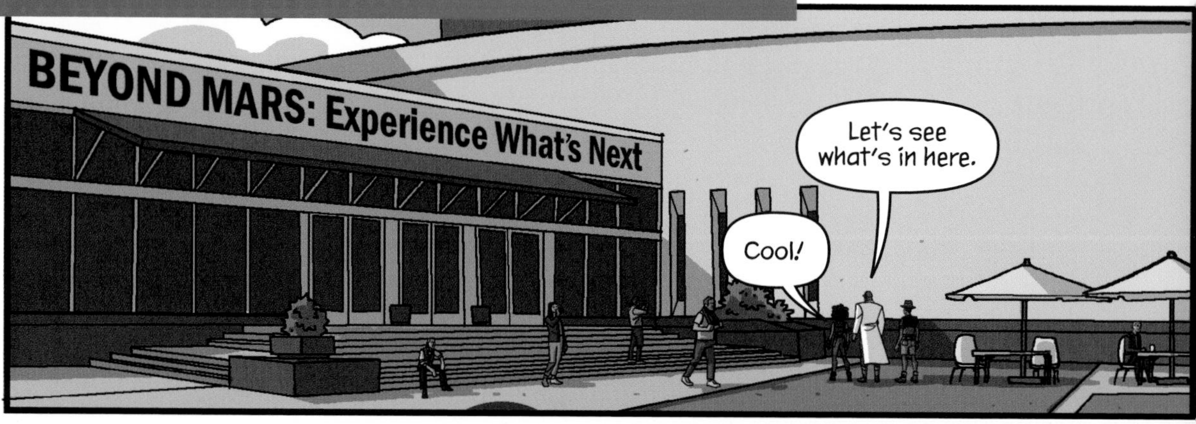
BEYOND MARS: Experience What's Next
Let's see what's in here.
Cool!

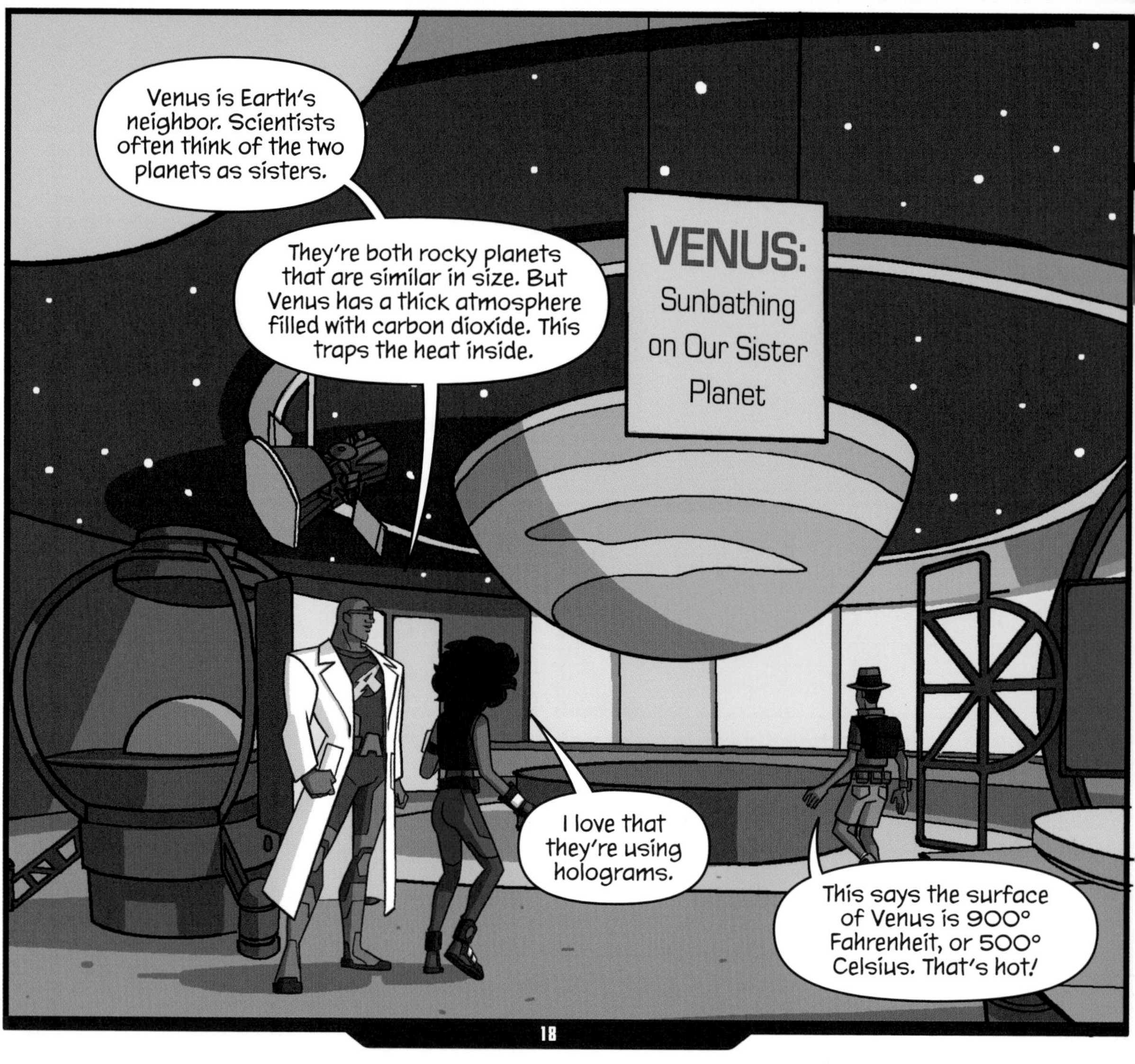
Venus is Earth's neighbor. Scientists often think of the two planets as sisters.
They're both rocky planets that are similar in size. But Venus has a thick atmosphere filled with carbon dioxide. This traps the heat inside.
VENUS: Sunbathing on Our Sister Planet
I love that they're using holograms.
This says the surface of Venus is 900° Fahrenheit, or 500° Celsius. That's hot!

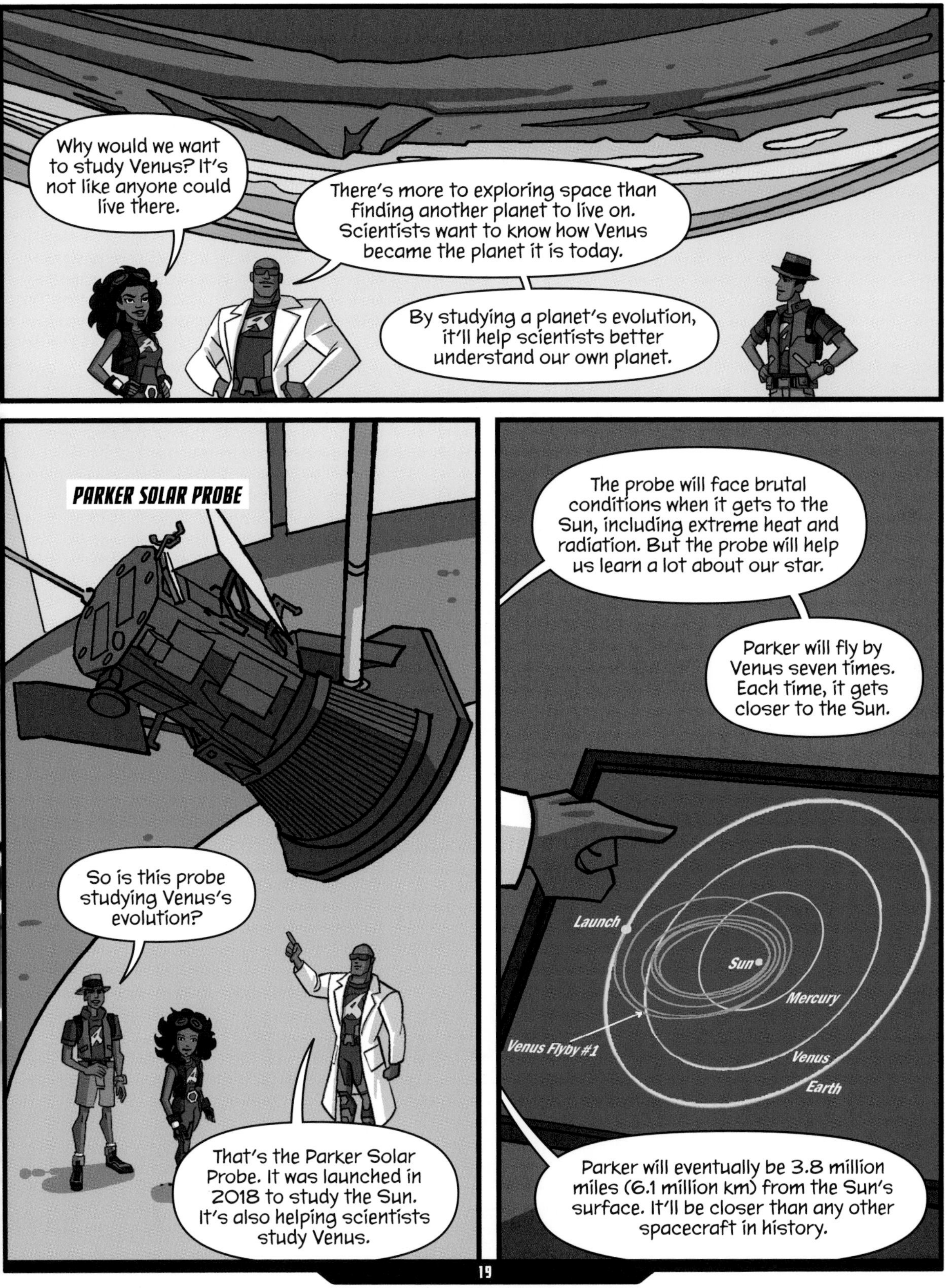
Why would we want to study Venus? It's not like anyone could live there.
There's more to exploring space than finding another planet to live on. Scientists want to know how Venus became the planet it is today.
By studying a planet's evolution, it'll help scientists better understand our own planet.
PARKER SOLAR PROBE
So is this probe studying Venus's evolution?
That's the Parker Solar Probe. It was launched in 2018 to study the Sun. It's also helping scientists study Venus.
The probe will face brutal conditions when it gets to the Sun, including extreme heat and radiation. But the probe will help us learn a lot about our star.
Parker will fly by Venus seven times. Each time, it gets closer to the Sun.
Launch
Sun
Mercury
Venus Flyby #1
Venus
Earth
Parker will eventually be 3.8 million miles (6.1 million km) from the Sun's surface. It'll be closer than any other spacecraft in history.

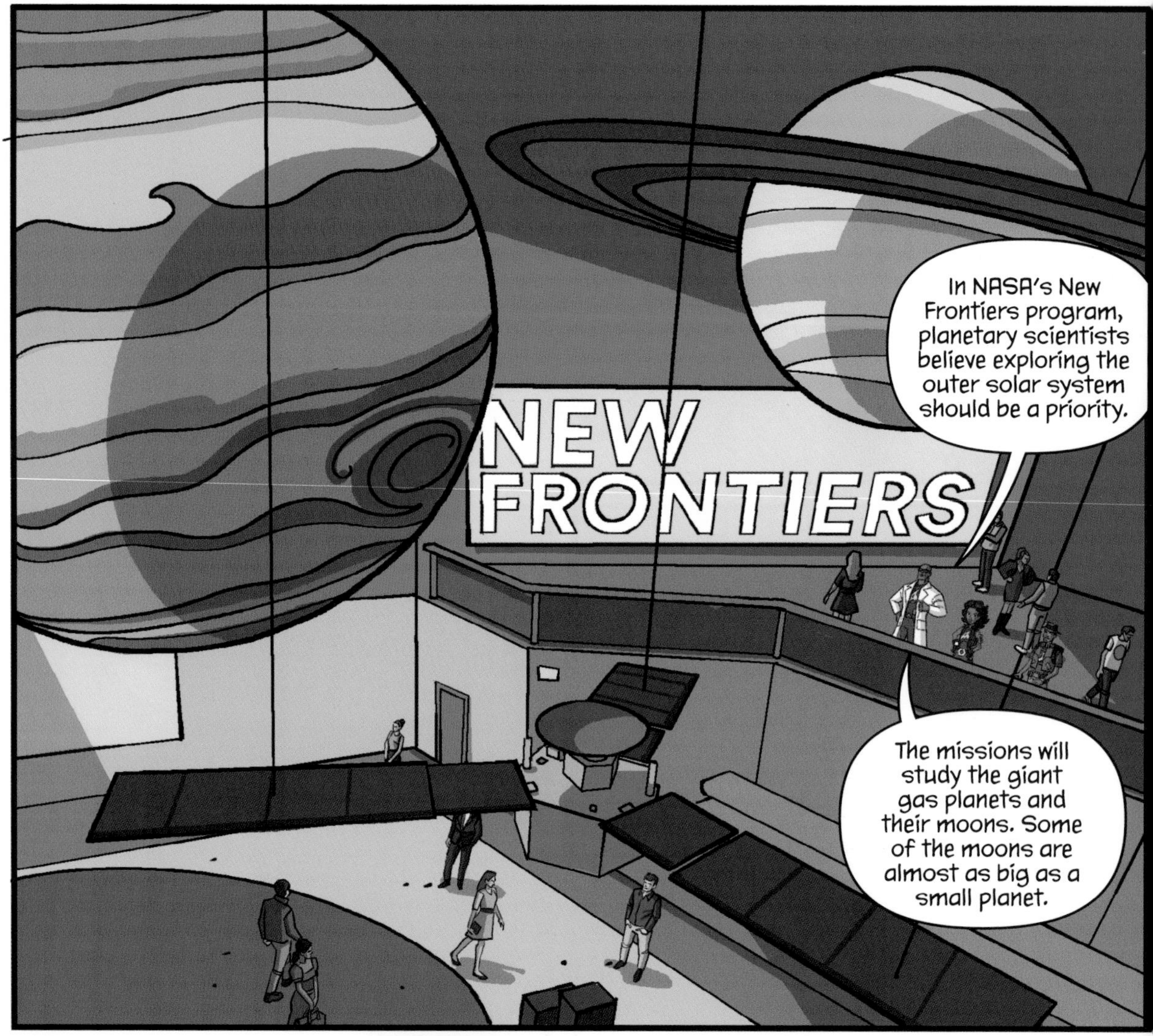
NEW FRONTIERS
In NASA's New Frontiers program, planetary scientists believe exploring the outer solar system should be a priority.
The missions will study the giant gas planets and their moons. Some of the moons are almost as big as a small planet.

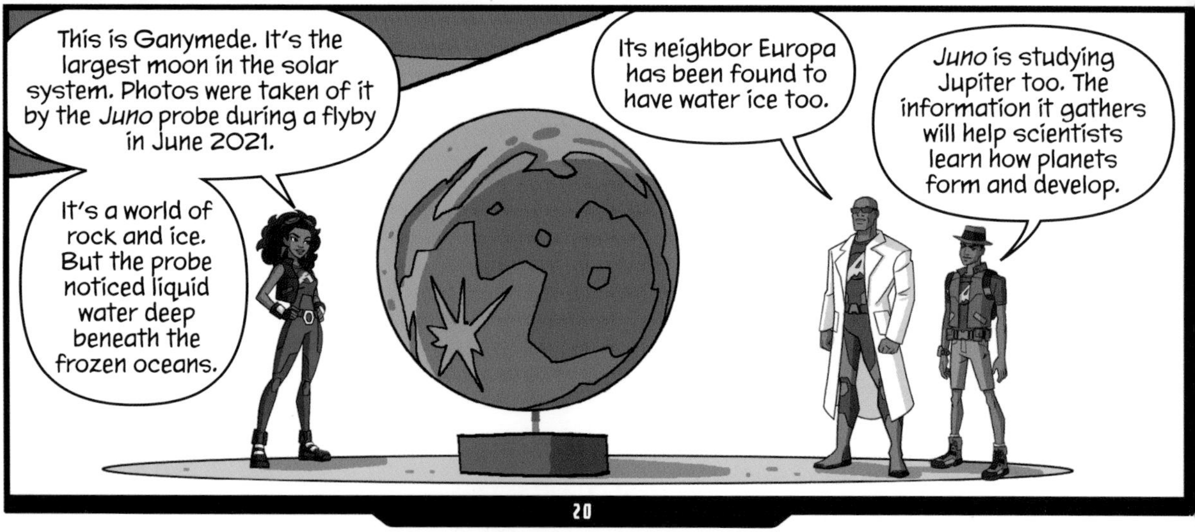
This is Ganymede. It's the largest moon in the solar system. Photos were taken of it by the *Juno* probe during a flyby in June 2021.
It's a world of rock and ice. But the probe noticed liquid water deep beneath the frozen oceans.
Its neighbor Europa has been found to have water ice too.
Juno is studying Jupiter too. The information it gathers will help scientists learn how planets form and develop.

This is a moon of Saturn. It's called Titan.

That's right. Titan has a thick atmosphere and heavy clouds. The surface can't be seen from space. So scientists are building a special craft called *Dragonfly*. It kind of looks like a robotic dragonfly, doesn't it?

Dragonfly will take samples on Titan's surface and do experiments to learn more about the moon. This mission is scheduled for 2026.

Why are we so interested in this moon? How is it different from the others?

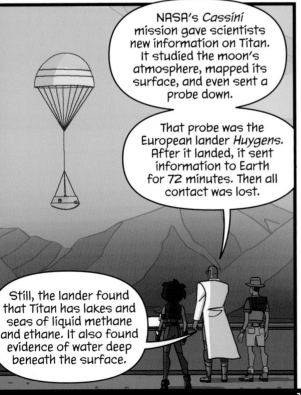

NASA's *Cassini* mission gave scientists new information on Titan. It studied the moon's atmosphere, mapped its surface, and even sent a probe down.

That probe was the European lander *Huygens*. After it landed, it sent information to Earth for 72 minutes. Then all contact was lost.

Still, the lander found that Titan has lakes and seas of liquid methane and ethane. It also found evidence of water deep beneath the surface.

Finding even traces of water on any other body in the solar system gives us hope that humans might survive out in space. That's why scientists are so interested in it.

So it's possible people could end up living on this moon, or on Ganymede. Amazing!

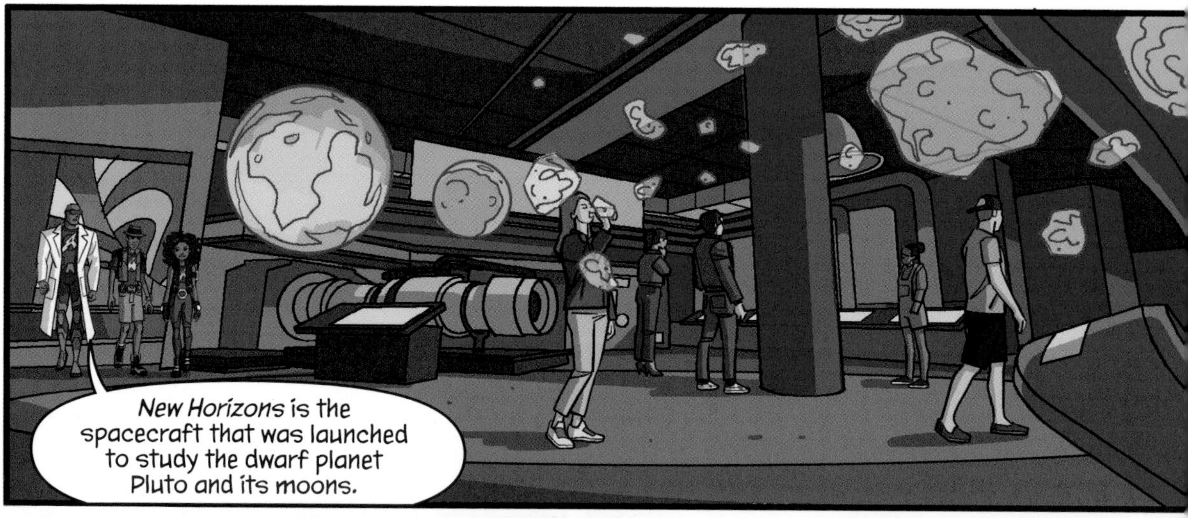
New Horizons is the spacecraft that was launched to study the dwarf planet Pluto and its moons.

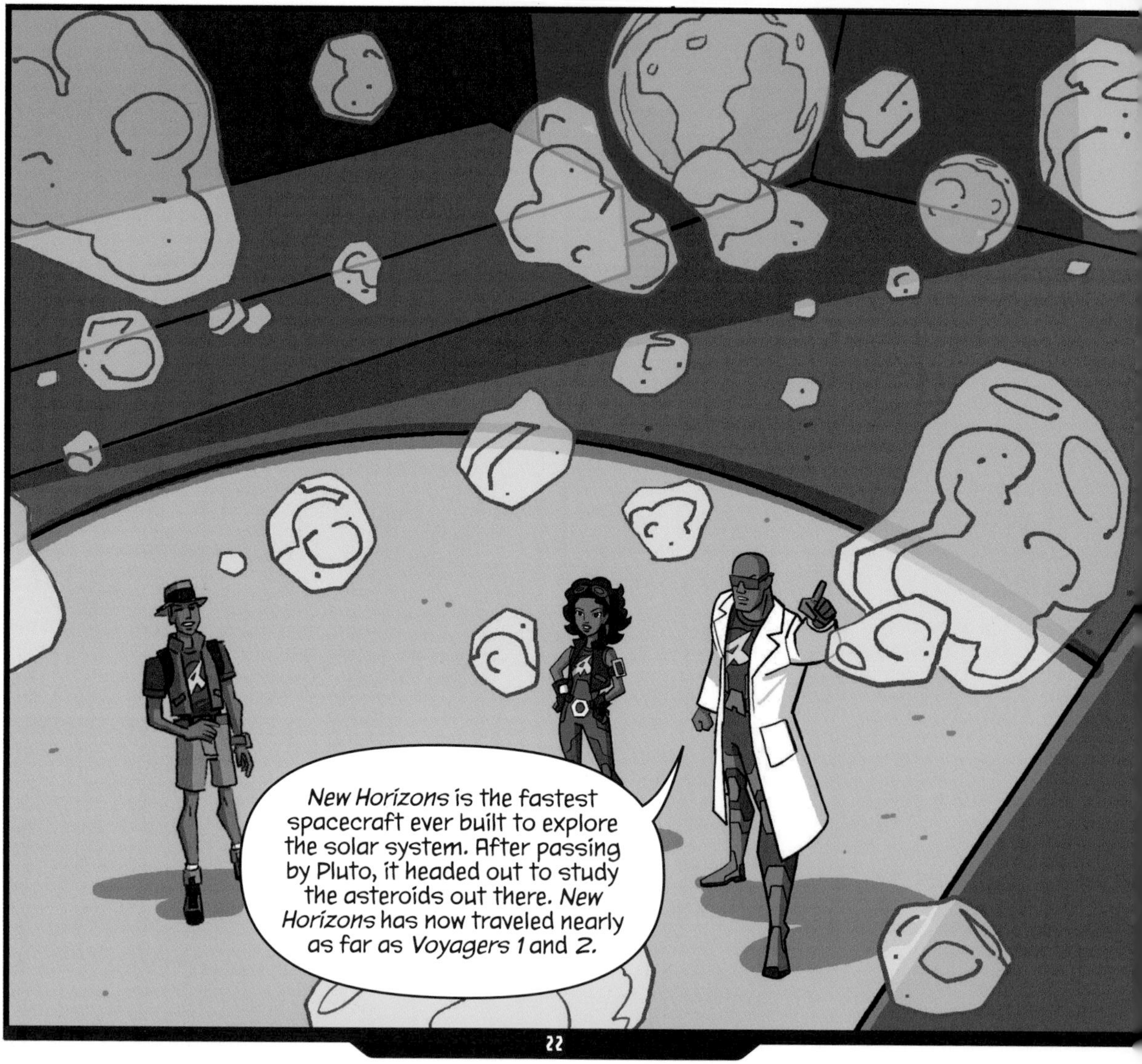
New Horizons is the fastest spacecraft ever built to explore the solar system. After passing by Pluto, it headed out to study the asteroids out there. New Horizons has now traveled nearly as far as Voyagers 1 and 2.

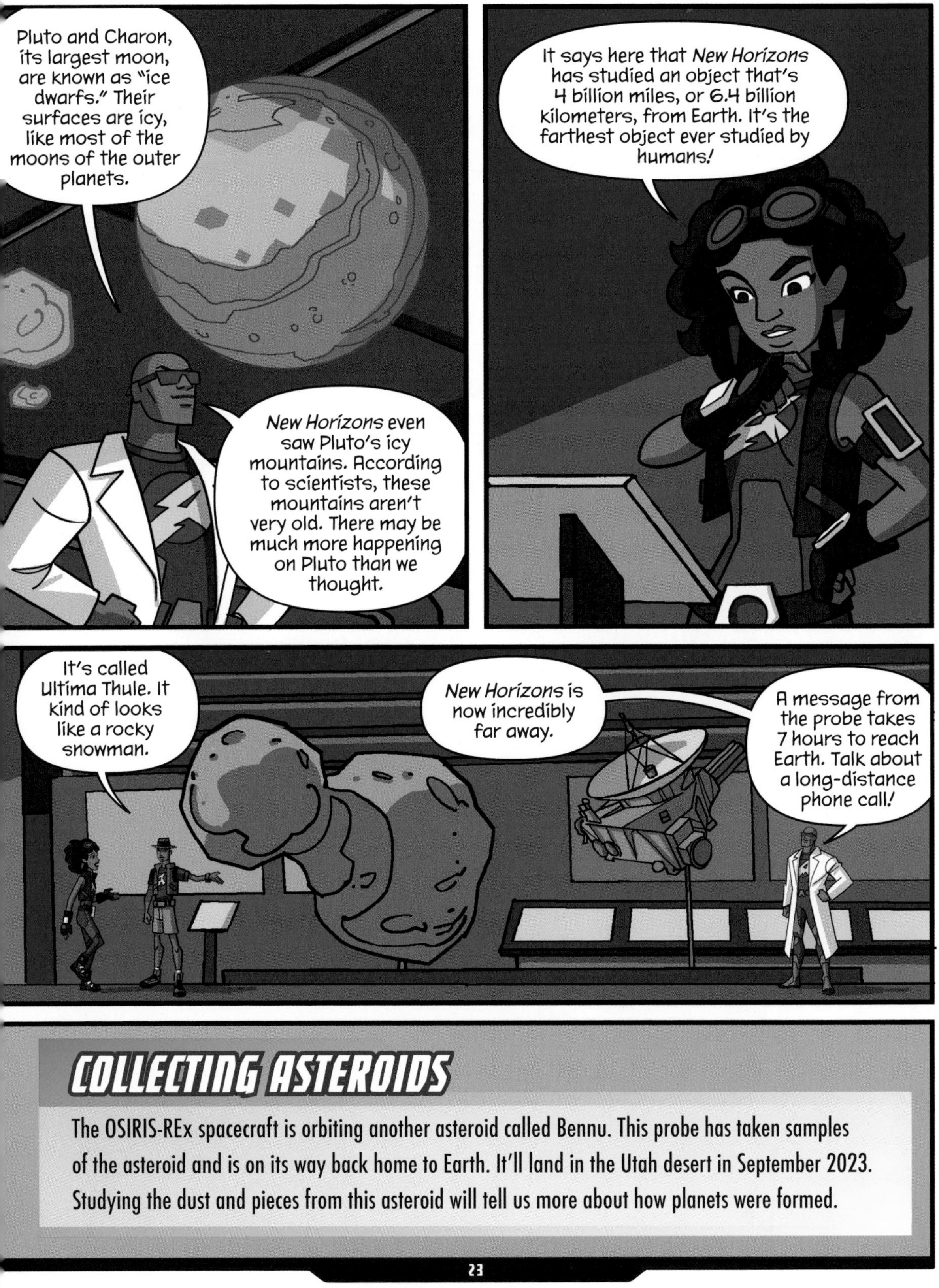
Pluto and Charon, its largest moon, are known as "ice dwarfs." Their surfaces are icy, like most of the moons of the outer planets.
New Horizons even saw Pluto's icy mountains. According to scientists, these mountains aren't very old. There may be much more happening on Pluto than we thought.
It says here that *New Horizons* has studied an object that's 4 billion miles, or 6.4 billion kilometers, from Earth. It's the farthest object ever studied by humans!
It's called Ultima Thule. It kind of looks like a rocky snowman.
New Horizons is now incredibly far away.
A message from the probe takes 7 hours to reach Earth. Talk about a long-distance phone call!

COLLECTING ASTEROIDS

The OSIRIS-REx spacecraft is orbiting another asteroid called Bennu. This probe has taken samples of the asteroid and is on its way back home to Earth. It'll land in the Utah desert in September 2023. Studying the dust and pieces from this asteroid will tell us more about how planets were formed.

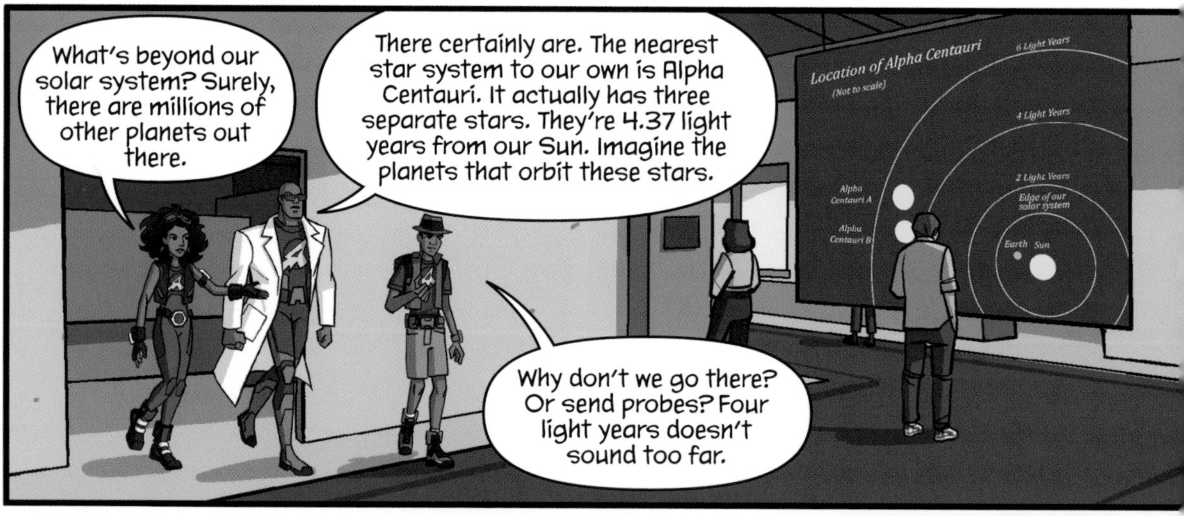
What's beyond our solar system? Surely, there are millions of other planets out there.
There certainly are. The nearest star system to our own is Alpha Centauri. It actually has three separate stars. They're 4.37 light years from our Sun. Imagine the planets that orbit these stars.
Location of Alpha Centauri
(Not to scale)
6 Light Years
4 Light Years
2 Light Years
Edge of our solar system
Alpha Centauri A
Alpha Centauri B
Earth
Sun
Why don't we go there? Or send probes? Four light years doesn't sound too far.
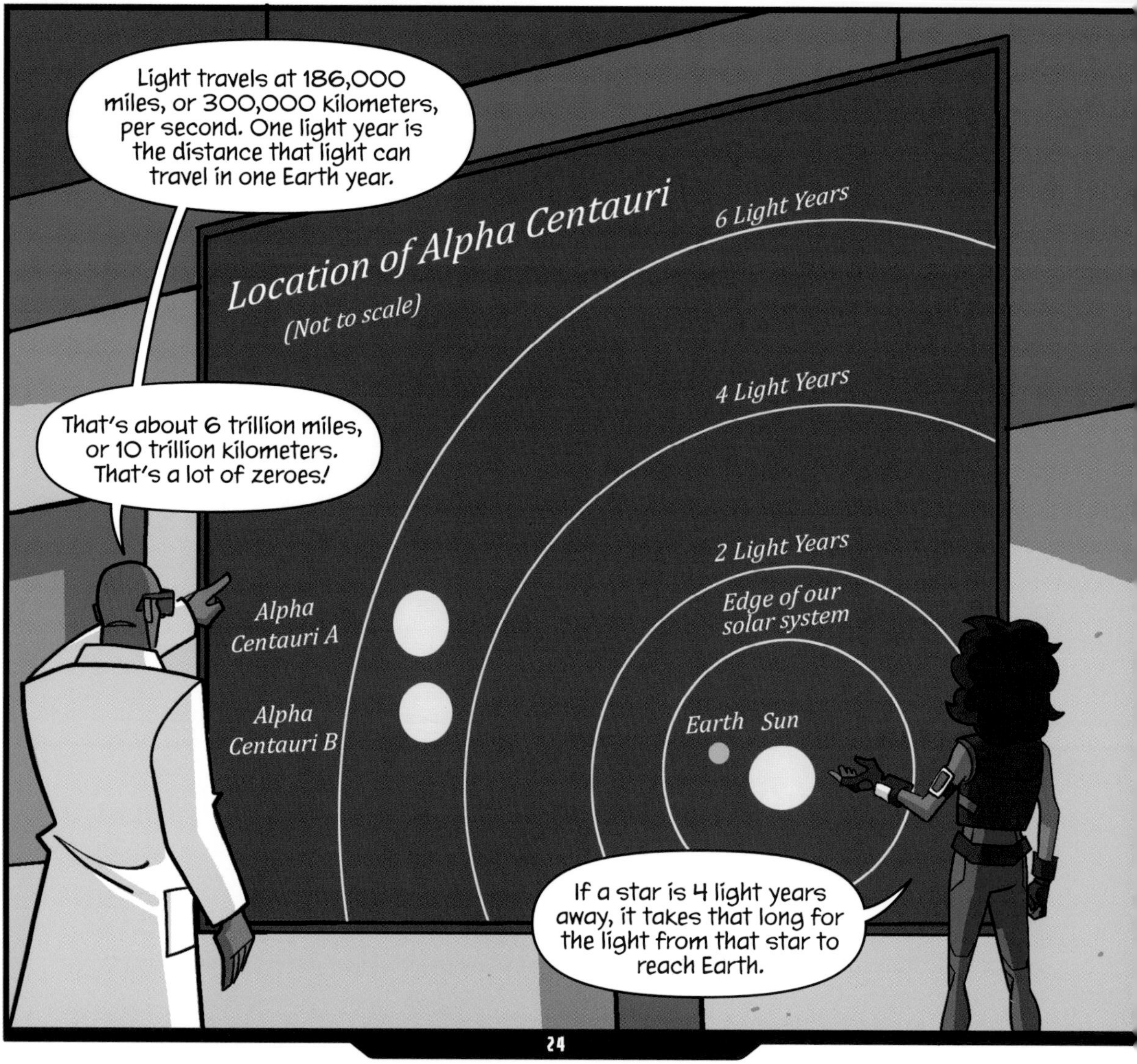
Light travels at 186,000 miles, or 300,000 kilometers, per second. One light year is the distance that light can travel in one Earth year.
Location of Alpha Centauri
(Not to scale)
6 Light Years
4 Light Years
2 Light Years
Edge of our solar system
Alpha Centauri A
Alpha Centauri B
Earth
Sun
That's about 6 trillion miles, or 10 trillion kilometers. That's a lot of zeroes!
If a star is 4 light years away, it takes that long for the light from that star to reach Earth.

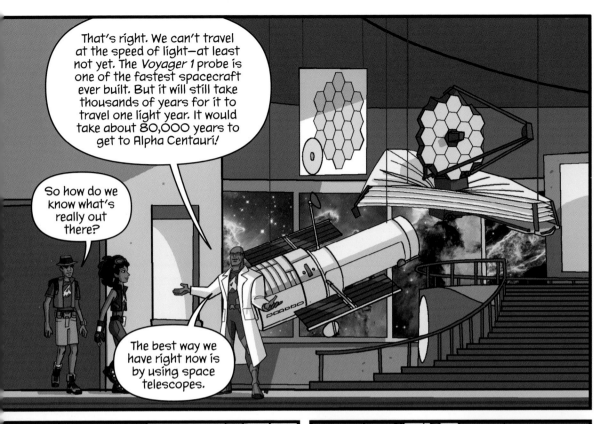

That's right. We can't travel at the speed of light—at least not yet. The *Voyager 1* probe is one of the fastest spacecraft ever built. But it will still take thousands of years for it to travel one light year. It would take about 80,000 years to get to Alpha Centauri!

So how do we know what's really out there?

The best way we have right now is by using space telescopes.

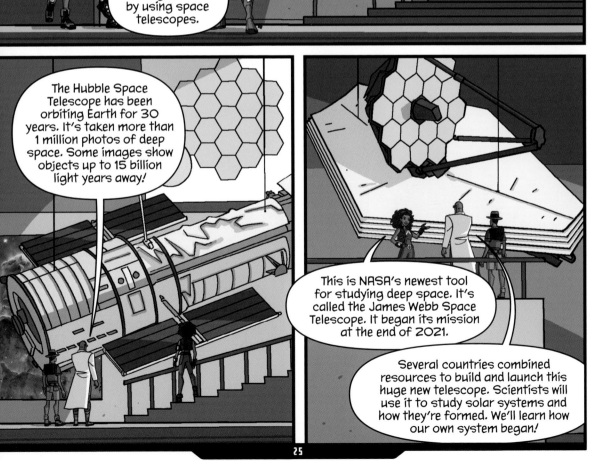

The Hubble Space Telescope has been orbiting Earth for 30 years. It's taken more than 1 million photos of deep space. Some images show objects up to 15 billion light years away!

This is NASA's newest tool for studying deep space. It's called the James Webb Space Telescope. It began its mission at the end of 2021.

Several countries combined resources to build and launch this huge new telescope. Scientists will use it to study solar systems and how they're formed. We'll learn how our own system began!

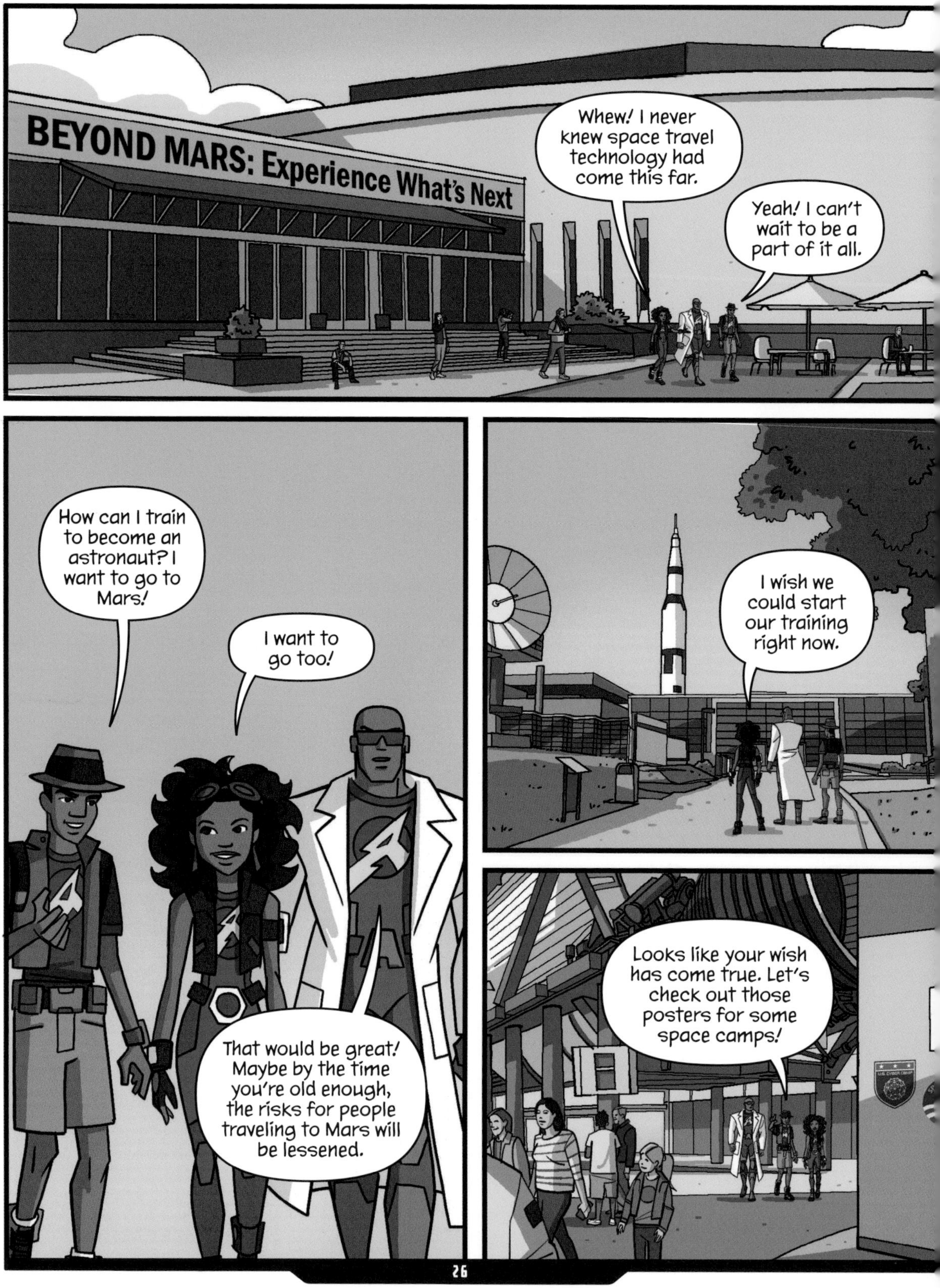
BEYOND MARS: Experience What's Next
Whew! I never knew space travel technology had come this far.
Yeah! I can't wait to be a part of it all.
How can I train to become an astronaut? I want to go to Mars!
I want to go too!
That would be great! Maybe by the time you're old enough, the risks for people traveling to Mars will be lessened.
I wish we could start our training right now.
Looks like your wish has come true. Let's check out those posters for some space camps!

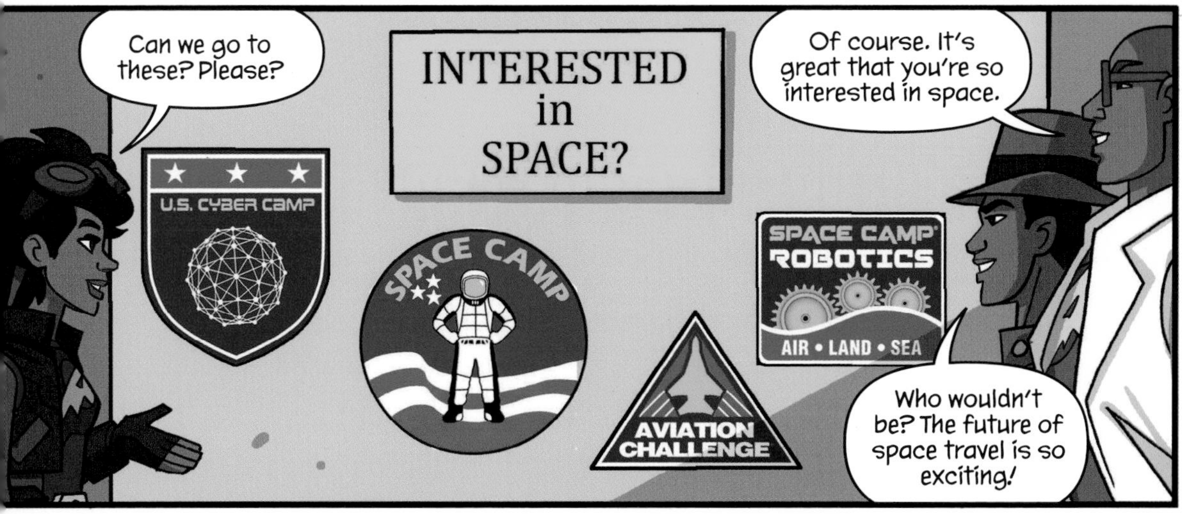
Can we go to these? Please?
INTERESTED in SPACE?
U.S. CYBER CAMP
SPACE CAMP
AVIATION CHALLENGE
SPACE CAMP ROBOTICS
AIR • LAND • SEA
Of course. It's great that you're so interested in space.
Who wouldn't be? The future of space travel is so exciting!

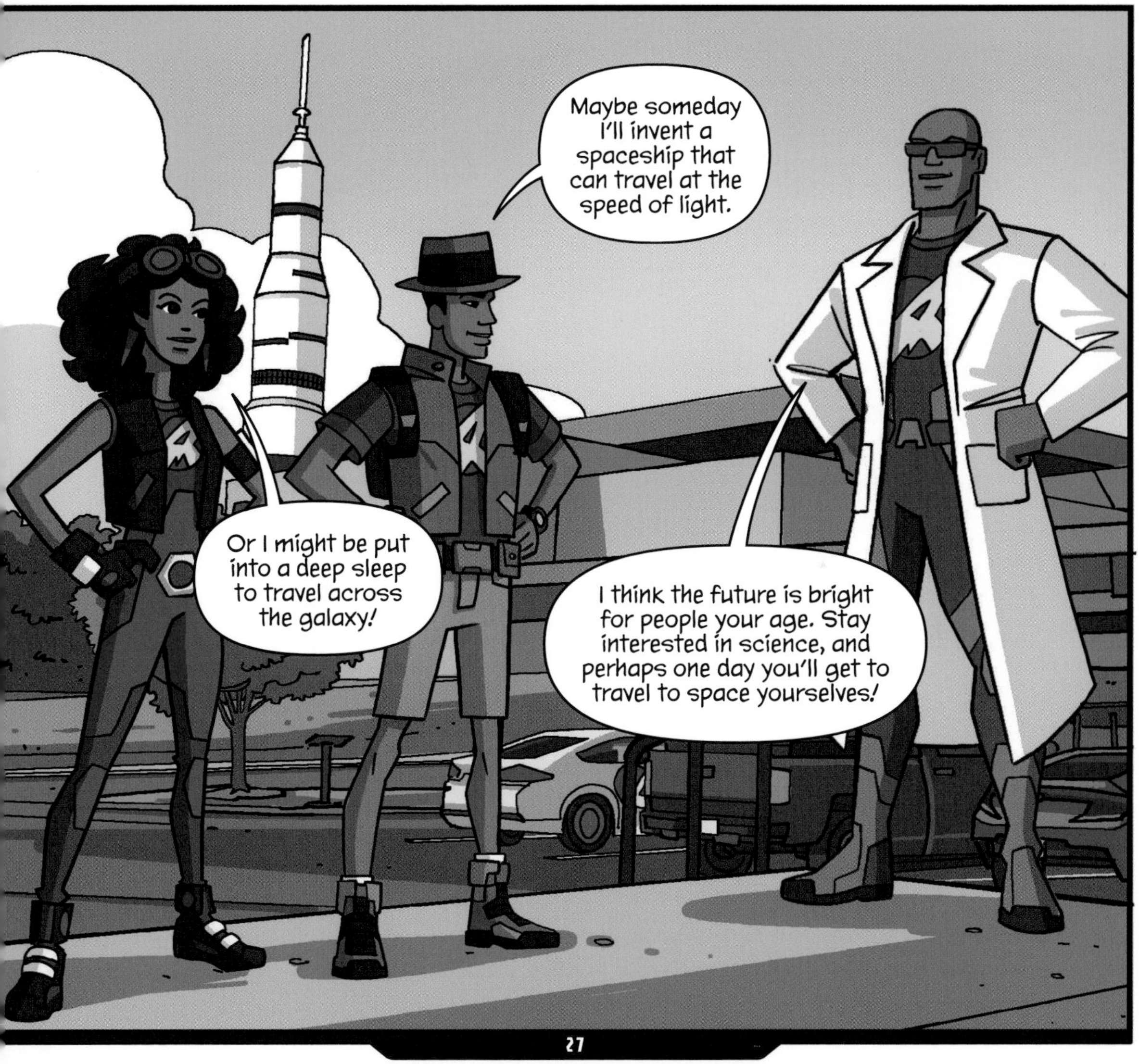
Maybe someday I'll invent a spaceship that can travel at the speed of light.
Or I might be put into a deep sleep to travel across the galaxy!
I think the future is bright for people your age. Stay interested in science, and perhaps one day you'll get to travel to space yourselves!

THE FUTURE OF SPACE EXPLORATION

Space is an enormous place. There are hundreds of moons, planets, and objects to study in our solar system alone. And there are countless others in other systems across the galaxy. People have long imagined what it would be like to travel into interstellar space. Many science fiction films and TV shows have told stories about visiting other worlds and meeting alien races.

Some of these stories may soon become reality. The most exciting and current mission is NASA's Artemis. Going back to Earth's moon would be only the first step toward moving on to Mars, Titan, or some other object in our solar system. Artemis will be a huge step in humanity's journey into deep space.

The future of space travel isn't just about going to new planets or moons. Space science can also help us learn about and care for our own planet. Satellites in orbit around Earth help study the planet's weather and learn about climate change.

Space tourism may soon be a big business. Companies are working to provide trips into space for average people so that anyone can experience weightlessness. Some companies are also planning to build space hotels that orbit Earth. They want to give people a whole new vacation experience.

Asteroid mining is another activity that scientists are interested in. Asteroids are giant rocks that orbit the Sun mainly between Mars and Jupiter. Many likely contain valuable metals and minerals. NASA has identified a few asteroids that might be mined. Scientists and engineers are working on new technology to accomplish this.

The Japanese space agency's mission, Hayabusa 2, has successfully landed a probe and two rovers on an asteroid. Samples of its material were brought back to Earth in December 2020. NASA's *Lucy* spacecraft was launched on October 16, 2021, to study asteroids that orbit the Sun on the same path as Jupiter. They're called Jupiter Trojans. Someday, space probes might bring home precious metals from these asteroids. Scientists estimate that these metals and minerals could be worth as much as $700 quintillion! With so much valuable material, asteroid mining could completely change the way we live on Earth.

GLOSSARY

atmosphere (AT-muh-sfeer)—the layer of gases that surrounds some planets, dwarf planets, and moons

automated (AW-tuh-mayt-uhd)—computer controlled or run by an automatic process

civilian (si-VIL-yuhn)—a person who is not a member of the military, police, firefighting, or astronaut forces

dehydrate (dee-HY-drayt)—the process of removing water from food to help preserve it

evolution (ev-uh-LOO-shuhn)—a gradual change in something over a long period of time

extract (ek-STRAKT)—to remove or take something out, especially by effort or force

hologram (HOL-uh-gram)—a three-dimensional (3D) image created using specialized beams of light

interchangeable (in-ter-CHAYN-juh-buhl)—the ability of two objects that can be used in place of each other

orbit (OR-bit)—to travel around an object in space; the path an object follows while circling an object in space

radiation (ray-dee-AY-shuhn)—waves or rays of energy sent out by sources of heat or light, or radioactive materials

remote-controlled (ri-MOHT-kuhn-TROHLD)—run by someone from a distance with a device that sends and receives radio signals

seismic (SIZE-mik)—having to do with ground movement resulting from an earthquake

READ MORE

Collins, Ailynn. *Probe Power: How Space Probes Do What Humans Can't.* North Mankato, MN: Capstone, 2020.

Goldstein, Margaret J. *Mysteries of Deep Space.* Minneapolis: Lerner Publishing, 2021.

Hubbard, Ben. *The Complete Guide to Space Exploration: A Journey of Discovery Across the Universe.* Oakland, CA: Lonely Planet Kids, 2020.

INTERNET SITES

NASA: Artemis Mission
nasa.gov/specials/artemis/

Sounds of Mars
mars.nasa.gov/mars2020/participate/sounds/?voice=true

Spacesuits for the Next Explorers
youtube.com/watch?v=vPkamuLqwM8

INDEX

Alpha Centauri, 24–25
Artemis mission, 10–11, 12, 28
asteroids, 22, 23
   mining of, 29
astronauts, 6, 7, 10, 11, 12, 16, 17, 26

dangers of space travel, 15–17

Hayabusa 2, 29

International Space Station (ISS), 7, 10, 16, 17
interstellar space, 9, 28

Kelly, Scott, 17

landers, 8, 9, 14, 15, 21
light years, 24–25

moons, 17, 20, 21, 22–23, 28
   the moon, 10, 11, 12, 13, 16, 28

NASA, 11, 14, 20, 21, 25, 28, 29
New Frontiers program, 20–21

orbiters, 8, 9

planets, 9, 18–19, 20, 22–23, 24, 28, 29
   Mars, 11, 13, 14–15, 16, 17, 26, 28, 29
probes, 8, 9, 10, 19, 20, 21, 22–23,
   24, 29
   Voyagers 1 and *2*, 8, 9, 22, 25

radiation, 16, 19
rovers, 14–15, 29

satellites, 28
space camps, 26–27
space suits, 13, 16
space telescopes, 25
space tourism, 7, 28
SpaceX, 11
speed of light, 24–25, 27
Sun, 19, 24, 29

Vande Hei, Mark, 17

water, 16, 17, 20, 21

ABOUT THE AUTHOR

Ailynn Collins has written several nonfiction children's books about amazing people, space, and science. Ailynn also loves to write fiction, especially stories about aliens, ghosts, witches, dinosaurs, and traveling through the universe. She lives outside Seattle, Washington with her husband and five dogs.

INTRODUCING ISSUES WITH

OPPOSING VIEWPOINTS®

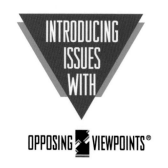

SMOKING

Other books in the Introducing Issues
with Opposing Viewpoints series:

AIDS
Alcohol
Civil Liberties
Cloning
The Death Penalty
Gangs
Gay Marriage
Genetic Engineering
Terrorism

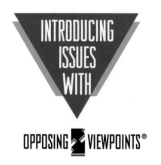

INTRODUCING ISSUES WITH

OPPOSING VIEWPOINTS®

SMOKING

Lauri S. Friedman, *Book Editor*

Bruce Glassman, *Vice President*
Bonnie Szumski, *Publisher, Series Editor*
Helen Cothran, *Managing Editor*

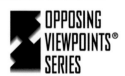

OPPOSING VIEWPOINTS® SERIES

GREENHAVEN PRESS
An imprint of Thomson Gale, a part of The Thomson Corporation

THOMSON GALE™

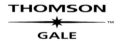

Detroit • New York • San Francisco • San Diego • New Haven, Conn. • Waterville, Maine • London • Munich

© 2006 Thomson Gale, a part of The Thomson Corporation.

Thomson and Star Logo are trademarks and Gale and Greenhaven Press are registered trademarks used herein under license.

For more information, contact
Greenhaven Press
27500 Drake Rd.
Farmington Hills, MI 48331-3535
Or you can visit our Internet site at http://www.gale.com

LIBRARY OF CONGRESS CATALOGING-IN-PUBLICATION DATA

Smoking / Lauri S. Friedman, book editor.
p. cm. — (Introducing issues with opposing viewpoints)
Includes bibliographical references and index.
ISBN 0-7377-3342-X (lib. : alk. paper)
1. Tobacco habit—United States. 2. Smoking—United States—Prevention.
3. Smoking—Health aspects—United States. 4. Smoking—Economic aspects—United States. I. Friedman, Lauri S. II. Series.
HV5760.S664 2006
362.29'6—dc22
2005046140

Printed in the United States of America